Test Yourself

Spanish Grammar

Julio López-Arias, Ph.D.
Department of Modern Languages and Literature
Ithaca College
Ithaca, NY

Gladys Varona-Lacey, Ph.D.
Department of Modern Languages and Literature
Ithaca College
Ithaca, NY

Contributing Editors

Steven M. DuPouy, Ph.D.
Department of Modern and Classical Languages
Georgia State University
Atlanta, GA

Ellen S. Haynes, Ph.D.
Department of Spanish and Portuguese
University of Colorado
Boulder, CO

Keith E. Watts, M.A.
Department of Spanish and Portuguese
University of New Mexico
Albuquerque, NM

NTC LearningWorks
a division of NTC Publishing Group
Lincolnwood, Illinois

Library of Congress Cataloging-in-Publication Data
is available from the Library of Congress.

A *Test Yourself Books, Inc.* Project

Contents

Preface

Test Yourself in Spanish Grammar has been designed and developed as a self-instructional and self-testing text that may also serve as a reference tool to review and supplement material presented in Spanish language courses.

The book is divided into two parts and contains a total of sixteen chapters. The first part tests the Spanish verbs, while the second part checks other important grammatical points. Each section within a chapter is introduced by a concise grammatical explanation and is accompanied by examples that illustrate the particular grammatical point being tested. The answers to the exercises appear at the end of each chapter to allow you to self-correct your work before continuing to the next unit within the chapter. The authors recommend that if you answer questions incorrectly, you should review the specific grammar point being tested before proceeding to the next unit.

Test Yourself in Spanish Grammar presents explanations of conceptual grammatical points in a logical fashion and provides self-test exercises that reinforce and facilitate the mastering of the essentials of Spanish grammar.

Julio López-Arias, Ph.D.
Gladys Varona-Lacey, Ph.D.
Department of Modern Languages and Literature
Ithaca College

How to Use this Book

This "Test Yourself" book is part of a unique series designed to help you improve your test scores on almost any type of examination you will face. Too often, you will study for a test—quiz, midterm, or final—and come away with a score that is lower than anticipated. Why? Because there is no way for you to really know how much you understand a topic until you've taken a test. The *purpose* of the test, after all, is to measure your complete understanding of the material.

The "Test Yourself" series offers you a way to improve your scores and to actually test your knowledge at the time you use this book. Consider each chapter a diagnostic pretest in a specific topic. Answer the questions, check your answers, and then give yourself a grade. Then, and only then, will you know where your strengths and, more important, weaknesses are. Once these areas are identified, you can strategically focus your study on those topics that need additional work.

Each book in this series presents a specific subject in an organized manner, and although each "Test Yourself" chapter may not correspond exactly to the same chapter in your textbook, you should have little difficulty in locating the specific topic you are studying. Written by educators in the field, each book is designed to correspond, as closely as possible, to the leading textbooks. This means that you can feel confident in using this book, and that regardless of your textbook, professor, or school, you will be much better prepared for anything you will encounter on your test.

Each chapter has four parts:

Brief Yourself. All chapters contain a brief overview of the topic that is intended to give you a more thorough understanding of the material with which you need to be familiar. Sometimes this information is presented at the beginning of the chapter, and sometimes it flows throughout the chapter, to review your understanding of various *units* within the chapter.

Test Yourself. Each chapter covers a specific topic corresponding to one that you will find in your textbook. Answer the questions, either on a separate page or directly in this book, if there is room.

Check Yourself. Check your answers. Every question is fully answered and explained. These answers will be the key to your increased understanding. If you answered the question incorrectly, read the explanations to *learn* and *understand* the material. You will note that at the end of every answer you will be referred to a specific subtopic within that chapter, so you can focus your studying and prepare more efficiently.

Grade Yourself. At the end of each chapter is a self-diagnostic key. By indicating on this form the numbers of those questions you answered incorrectly, you will have a clear picture of your weak areas.

There are no secrets to test success. Only good preparation can guarantee high grades. By utilizing this "Test Yourself" book, you will have a better chance of improving your scores and understanding the subject more fully.

Part I:
Verbs

The Indicative Mood: The Present Tense

Brief Yourself

The present indicative is used to state what is universally true or true in the present. It is also used to express a future action if such is indicated by a word or a phrase in the sentence.

Test Yourself

1.1 *-ar* verbs. Stem endings:

yo	-o	nosotros (as)	-amos
tú	-as	vosotros (as)	-áis
usted	-a	ustedes	-an
él	-a	ellos	-an
ella	-a	ellas	-an

Example:

yo	estudio
tú	estudias
usted	estudia
él	estudia
ella	estudia
nosotros (as)	estudiamos
vosotros (as)	estudiáis
ustedes	estudian
ellos	estudian
ellas	estudian

Exercises: Fill in the blanks with the present indicative of the verbs in parentheses.

1. Yo _____ francés en la universidad. (estudiar)

2. Tú _____ la televisión todas las noches. (mirar)

3. Ustedes _____ en la universidad. (enseñar)

4. Vosotros _____ la ropa los sábados. (lavar)

5. Mi padre _____en un hospital. (trabajar)

6. Ella _____ sus libros en la librería de la universidad. (comprar)

7. Los chicos _____ a las chicas a la fiesta del viernes. (invitar)

8. Él _____ a Colombia todos los años. (viajar)

9. Nosotros _____ en el restaurante japonés. (cenar)

10. Tú _____la luz cuando sales. (apagar)

11. Los padres de mi amigo _____ las cuentas. (pagar)

12. Yo _____ a mis padres todos los meses. (visitar)

13. El estudiante nunca _____. (cocinar)

14. Emilio _____ muy bien. (cantar)

15. María y Juan _____ en todas las fiestas. (bailar)

16. Ellas _____ en las montañas. (esquiar)

17. Vosotros _____ en el mar. (nadar)

18. Nosotros _____cuando vemos una película triste. (llorar)

1.2   -er verbs. Stem endings:

yo	-o	nosotros (as)	-emos
tú	-es	vosotros (as)	-éis
usted	-e	ustedes	-en
él	-e	ellos	-en
ella	-e	ellas	-en

Example:

yo	como
tú	comes
usted	come
él	come
ella	come
nosotros (as)	comemos
vosotros (as)	coméis
ustedes	comen
ellos	comen
ellas	comen

Exercises: Fill in the blanks with the present indicative of the verbs in parentheses.

1. Yo _____ mucha fruta todos los días. (comer)

2. Ustedes _____ que él es importante. (creer)

3. Tú _____ a patinar en el hielo. (aprender)

4. Nosotros _____ en restaurantes chinos. (comer)

5. Él _____ venir temprano. (prometer)

6. Ustedes _____ jugo de naranja. (beber)

7. Vosotros _____ coches extranjeros. (vender)

8. Ella _____ las películas románticas. (ver)

9. Los chicos _____ por el jardín. (correr)

10. Ella _____a las cartas. (responder)

11. Nosotras _____ mucho dinero. (deber)

12. Tú _____ el periódico todos los días. (leer)

1.3 *-ir* verbs. Stem endings:

yo	-o	nosotros (as)	-imos
tú	-es	vosotros (as)	-ís
usted	-e	ustedes	-en
él	-e	ellos	-en
ella	-e	ellas	-en

Example:

yo	-abro
tú	-abres
usted	-abre
él	-abre
ella	-abre
nosotros (as)	-abrimos
vosotros (as)	-abrís
ellos	-abren
ellas	-abren

Exercises: Fill in the blanks with the present indicative of the verbs in parentheses.

1. Nosotros _____ los regalos. (abrir)

2. Él _____ que hace frío. (admitir)

3. Ellos _____ la escalera. (subir)

4. Yo _____ lejos de aquí. (vivir)

5. Tú _____ a los pobres. (asistir)

6. Usted _____ noticias de la familia. (recibir)

7. Vosotros _____ cartas a los amigos. (escribir)

8. Felipe _____ con su padre. (discutir)

9. Los estudiantes _____ al presidente. (aplaudir)

10. Vosotras _____ la información. (omitir)

11. Él _____ la comida con un plato. (cubrir)

12. Ustedes _____ cómo vamos a ir. (decidir)

13. Nosotras _____ cartas a nuestros amigos. (escribir)

1.4 Stem-changing verbs

Changes occur in the stressed syllables of the verbs in all forms except *nosotros* and *vosotros*.

a) *e* changes to *ie*

-ar verbs	*-er* verbs	*-ir* verbs
cerrar	*entender*	*mentir*
cierro	entiendo	miento
cierras	entiendes	mientes
cierra	entiende	miente
cerramos	entendemos	mentimos
cerráis	entendéis	mentís
cierran	entienden	mienten

b) *o* to *ue*

-ar verbs	*-er* verbs	*-ir* verbs
volar	*volver*	*dormir*
vuelo	vuelvo	duermo
vuelas	vuelves	duermes
vuela	vuelve	duerme
volamos	volvemos	dormimos

voláis   volvéis   dormís

vuelan   vuelves   duermen

c) *u* to *ue*

    jugar: juego, juegas, juega, jugamos, jugáis, juegan

d) *e* to *i* (*-ir* verbs only)

    pedir: pido, pides, pide, pedimos, pedís, piden

Exercises: Fill in the blanks with the present indicative of the verbs in parethesis.

1. El profesor _____ la puerta de la clase. (cerrar)

2. La fiesta _____ muy tarde. (empezar)

3. Las vacaciones _____ la semana que viene. (comenzar)

4. Yo _____ mucho en mi futuro. (pensar)

5. El gobernador _____ sin problemas. (gobernar)

6. Ustedes _____ el café por las mañanas. (calentar)

7. Ella _____ siempre a su amigo. (defender)

8. A veces yo _____ el autobús. (perder)

9. Ustedes _____ estudiar por la noche. (preferir)

10. Yo no _____ los sentimientos de mis amigos. (herir)

11. Ellos _____ mucho antes de ir a clase. (dormir)

12. Yo _____ al Caribe todos los años. (volar)

13. Mis amigos _____ muchas historias. (contar)

14. Tú no _____ la salida de la residencia. (encontrar)

15. Ellos _____ todas las comidas. (probar)

16. Ustedes _____ a su cuarto después de cenar. (volver)

17. El perro de mi vecino _____. (morder)

18. Yo _____ estudiar antes de los exámenes. (soler)

19. Ellos se _____ por ir a Portugal. (morir)

20. Vosotros _____ ayuda cuando la necesitáis. (pedir)

21. El maestro no _____ las preguntas. (repetir)

22. En clase nosotros nos _____ mucho. (reír)

23. Yo _____ al fútbol y al baloncesto. (jugar)

1.5 Verbs with orthographic changes

Orthographic changes occur in some verbs in the first person singular and plural, and in the second person plural.

a) Changes occur only in the first person singular.

g changes to *j*   corregir: corrijo

c changes to *z*   convencer: convenzo

c changes to *zc* before *a* or *o* conocer: conozco

b) Changes occur in all persons except *nosotros* and *vosotros*.

i changes to *y*   *construir:* construyo, construyes, construye, construimos, construís, construyen

Exercises: Fill in the blanks with the present indicative of the verbs in parentheses.

1. Yo _____ los exámenes. (corregir)

2. Nosotros _____ más clases fáciles que difíciles. (escoger)

3. Yo _____ a mis compañeros. (proteger)

4. Tú _____ la mesa después de comer. (recoger)

5. Yo _____ con mis explicaciones. (convencer)

6. Las fiestas _____ muy temprano. (comenzar)

7. Yo _____ del inglés al español. (traducir)

8. Yo _____ en clase todos los días. (aparecer)

9. Tú _____ con tus impuestos. (contribuir)

10. Yo nunca _____ borracho. (conducir)

11. Los obreros _____ muchos edificios. (construir)

12. Yo no _____ a ningún estudiante internacional. (conocer)

1.6   Other irregularities

a)   Verbs with changes that occur only in the first person singular:

poner:	pongo
salir:	salgo
saber:	sé
hacer:	hago
caer:	caigo
dar:	doy
caber:	quepo

b)   The stem of the following verbs changes in all forms except *nosotros* and *vosotros*. These verbs also have an irregular first person:

tener	*venir*	*oír*	*decir*
tengo	vengo	oigo	digo
tienes	vienes	oyes	dices
tiene	viene	oye	dice
tenemos	venimos	oímos	decimos
tenéis	venís	oís	decís
tienen	vienen	oyen	dicen

c)   Verbs that have changes in all persons:

ir	*haber**
voy	he
vas	has
va	ha
vamos	hemos
vais	habéis
van	han

*The verb *haber* has the impersonal form *hay* in the third person singular and plural.

Exercises: Fill in the blanks with the present indicative of the verbs in parentheses.

1. Los estudiantes _____ mucho tiempo libre. (tener)

2. Yo _____ toda mi ropa en el suelo. (poner)

3. Nosotros _____ siempre tarde a las reuniones. (venir)

4. Yo _____ regalos a mis padres. (dar)

5. Ella no _____ lo que dice el profesor. (oír)

6. Yo no _____ en esta silla. (caber)

7. Yo _____ todas las preguntas del examen. (saber)

8. Nosotros _____ misa todos los domingos. (oír)

9. Yo _____ siempre la verdad. (decir)

10. Tú _____ a la biblioteca cada dos días. (ir)

11. Yo no me _____ en el hielo. (caer)

12. Yo _____ de casa muy tarde. (salir)

13. María nunca _____ mentiras. (decir)

14. Todos ustedes _____ dinero constantemente. (pedir)

✓ Check Yourself

1.1 (*-ar* verbs)

1. estudio 2. miras 3. enseñan 4. laváis 5. trabaja 6. compra 7. invitan 8. viaja 9. cenamos 10. apagas 11. pagan 12. visito 13. cocina 14. canta 15. bailan 16. esquían 17. nadáis 18. lloramos

1.2 (*-er* verbs)

1. como 2. creen 3. aprendes 4. comemos 5. promete 6. beben 7. vendéis 8. ve 9. corren 10. responde 11. debemos 12. lees

1.3 (*-ir* verbs)

1. abrimos 2. admite 3. suben 4. vivo 5. asistes 6. recibe 7. escribís 8. discute 9. aplauden 10. omitís 11. cubre 12. deciden 13. escribimos

1.4 (Stem-changing verbs)

1. cierra 2. empieza 3. comienzan 4. pienso 5. gobierna 6. calientan 7. defiende 8. pierdo 9. prefieren 10. hiero 11. duermen 12. vuelo 13. cuentan 14. encuentras 15. prueban 16. vuelven 17. muerde 18. suelo 19. mueren 20. pedís 21. repite 22. reímos 23. juego

1.5 (Verbs with orthographic changes)

1. corrijo 2. escogemos 3. protejo 4. recoges 5. convenzo 6. comienzan 7. traduzco 8. aparezco 9. contribuyes 10. conduzco 11. construyen 12. conozco

1.6 (Other irregularities)

1. tienen 2. pongo 3. venimos 4. doy 5. oye 6. quepo 7. sé 8. oímos 9. digo 10. vas 11. caigo 12. salgo 13. dice 14. piden

Grade Yourself

Circle the numbers of the questions you missed, then fill in the total incorrect for each topic. If you answered more than three questions incorrectly, you need to focus on that topic. (If a topic has less than three questions and you had at least one wrong, we suggest you study that topic also. Read your textbook, a review book, or ask your teacher for help.)

Subject: The Indicative Mood: The Present Tense

Topic	Question Numbers	Number Incorrect
-*ar* verbs	**1.1:** 1, 2, 3, 4, 5, 6, 7, 8, 9, 10, 11, 12, 13, 14, 15, 16, 17, 18	
-*er* verbs	**1.2:** 1, 2, 3, 4, 5, 6, 7, 8, 9, 10, 11, 12	
-*ir* verbs	**1.3:** 1, 2, 3, 4, 5, 6, 7, 8, 9, 10, 11, 12, 13	
Stem-changing verbs	**1.4:** 1, 2, 3, 4, 5, 6, 7, 8, 9, 10, 11, 12, 13, 14, 15, 16, 17, 18, 19, 20, 21, 22, 23	
Verbs with orthographic changes	**1.5:** 1, 2, 3, 4, 5, 6, 7, 8, 9, 10, 11, 12	
Other irregularities	**1.6:** 1, 2, 3, 4, 5, 6, 7, 8, 9, 10, 11, 12, 13, 14	

The Indicative Mood: The Past and Future Tenses

2

Brief Yourself

Spanish has two simple past tenses: the preterite and the imperfect. Both refer to past actions with regard to the present. The future tense refers to an action that will take place at a future time.

Test Yourself

2.1 The preterite

The preterite refers to an action completed in the past. It is used to describe an event that took place within a limited period of time and its beginning and/or end is indicated. The preterite is formed by adding the preterite endings to the stem of the infinitive.

hablar	→	habl-	+	preterite ending
comer	→	com-	+	preterite ending
vivir	→	viv-	+	preterite ending

-ar	*-er*	*-ir*
-é	-í	-í
-aste	-iste	-iste
-ó	-ió	-ió
-amos	-imos	-imos
-asteis	-isteis	-isteis
-aron	-ieron	-ieron

-er and *-ir* verbs whose stems end in a vowel have a spelling change in the third person singular and plural forms. The *-ió* and *-ieron* endings are spelled *-yó* and *-yeron* (E.g.: *creer: creyó, creyeron; oír: oyó, oyeron*).

Example:

La visité la semana pasada.
I visited her last week.

Exercises: Write the appropriate preterite form of the verbs in parentheses.

1. Ayer ella _____ con el presidente. (hablar)

2. Durante las vacaciones yo _____ todos los días en el mismo restaurante. (comer)

3. Ustedes se _____ por la multa. (pelear)

4. Tú me _____ los documentos. (exigir)

5. Nosotros _____ la información anoche. (recibir)

6. Usted _____ a las dos de la mañana. (salir)

7. Ellos _____ la casa antes de venderla. (barrer)

8. Vosotros _____ artículos interesantes. (escribir)

9. Las estudiantes _____ a estudiar temprano. (empezar)

10. La chica _____ la noticia. (creer)

11. Ellos _____ los gritos de la mujer. (oír)

2.1.1 Irregular preterites

Irregular preterite verbs have irregularities in the stem and the endings.

verb	stem	ending	
estar	estuv-		
andar	anduv-		
tener	tuv-	-e	
		-iste	
poder	pud-	-o	
poner	pus-	-imos	
saber	sup-	-isteis	
		-ieron	
querer	quis-		
hacer	hic-*		
venir	vin-		
traer	traj-	-e	-imos
decir	dij-	-iste	-isteis
producir	produj-	-o	-eron

c to *z* in the third person singular: *hizo*

Other irregular verbs:

dar: di, diste, dio, dimos, disteis, dieron

ir/ser: fui, fuiste, fue, fuimos, fuisteis, fueron

haber: hubo (*there was*)

Exercises: Write the appropriate preterite form of the verbs in parentheses.

1. Yo _____ en la Florida varias veces. (estar)

2. Carlos _____ por el parque toda la mañana. (andar)

3. Hoy usted _____ un examen de literatura griega. (tener)

4. Los chicos _____ los pasaportes y los cheques de viajeros. (traer)

5. Ustedes _____ el dinero en una cuenta de ahorros. (poner)

6. Tú no _____ aceptar la invitación al concierto. (poder)

7. Nosotros no _____ que él supiera la noticia. (querer)

8. _____ muchos invitados en la recepción del canciller. (Haber)

9. ¿Por qué vosotros no _____ a México con vuestros padres? (ir)

10. El director _____ una película excelente. (producir)

11. Las hermanas les _____ todo a sus padres. (decir)

12. Ella _____ a mi casa después de cenar. (venir)

13. Mercedes _____ la mejor estudiante de su curso. (ser)

2.1.2 Preterite of *-ir* stem-changing verbs

All the *-ir* verbs that have stem changes in the present tense also have changes in the third person singular and plural: *o > u* and *e > i*.

dormir: dormí, dormiste, d*u*rmió, dormimos, dormisteis, d*u*rmieron

pedir: pedí, pediste, pidió, pedimos,
           pedisteis, pidieron

Example:

Los niños durmieron en casa de sus amigos.
The children slept at their friends' house.

Exercises: Write the appropriate preterite form of
the verbs in parentheses.

1. El arzobispo _____ el año pasado. (morir)

2. Ustedes no _____ bien anoche. (dormir)

3. Yo _____ la película italiana sin
   problemas. (seguir)

4. Ella _____ marcharse antes de las doce
   de la noche. (preferir).

5. Nosotros no _____ el empleo que
   deseamos. (conseguir)

6. Los parientes de Jorge _____ quedarse en
   un hotel de lujo. (preferir)

7. Alberto y Enrique _____ una botella de
   vino tinto. (pedir)

8. Anoche me _____ a las diez. (dormir)

9. Ellos los _____ hasta que llegaron al
   aeropuerto. (seguir)

10. Vosotras _____ de comer lo mismo
    que ellos. (pedir)

2.2.1   The imperfect

The imperfect refers to progressive actions in the past
that were going on for an indefinite period of time. It is
used to describe continued, habitual, or repeated actions
in the past and provides background information such
as time, weather, age, outward and physical appearances,
feelings, beliefs, and emotional states. The imperfect is
translated into English as *used to*, *was* (*were*) + *-ing*, and

would. To form the imperfect, the following endings are
added to the stem of the verb:

-*ar* verbs	-*er* and -*ir* verbs
-aba	-ía
-abas	-ías
-aba	-ía
-ábamos	-íamos
-abais	-ías
-aban	-ían

The Spanish imperfect is equivalent to three English
forms:

Yo trabajaba en Madrid.
I used to work in Madrid.
I was working in Madrid.
I worked in Madrid.

Exercises: Write the correct form of the imperfect of
the verbs in parentheses.

1. Los senadores _____ de política en sus
   fiestas. (discutir)

2. Roberto siempre _____ un auto deportivo.
   (conducir)

3. Mis amigas _____ siempre a la
   entrenadora en el gimnasio. (visitar)

4. Durante los veranos yo _____ al
   extranjero. (viajar)

5. Mis compañeros de cuarto _____ con
   frecuencia. (esquiar)

6. El presidente _____ a las reuniones del
   congreso. (asistir)

7. Tú te _____ temprano durante la semana.
   (levantar)

8. Vosotras _____ la conferencia
   internacional. (organizar)

9. El profesor Suárez siempre _____ chistes en sus clases. (contar)

10. El padre _____ con el profesor de su hijo. (platicar)

11. Cuando llegamos a casa, ella no _____. (estar)

12. Mi hija menor _____ dos años cuando nos mudamos a Venezuela. (tener)

13. Su prima Isabel se _____ cuando sacaba malas notas. (deprimir)

14. Julio y Nancy _____ mucho en las fiestas. (bailar)

15. María y Pedro no _____ mucho cuando _____. (gastar, viajar)

2.2.2 Irregular imperfect

Only three verbs have an irregular form in the imperfect—*ir*, *ser*, and *ver*:

    ir: iba, ibas, iba, íbamos, ibais, iban

    ser: era, eras, era, éramos, érais, eran

    ver: veía, veías, veía, veíamos, veíais, veían

Exercises: Write the correct form of the imperfect of the verbs in parentheses.

1. Él _____ la persona adecuada para el puesto. (ser)

2. Nosotros nunca _____ al campo durante los inviernos. (ir)

3. Joaquín _____ a sus socios todas las noches. (ver)

4. Emilio y yo _____ buenos amigos. (ser)

5. Ustedes se _____ pocas veces cuando _____ novios. (ver, ser)

6. Tú _____ muy irresponsable cuando _____ pequeña. (ser, ser)

7. Yo _____ en Cuba cuando _____ niña. (vivir, ser)

8. Todos los fines de semanas yo _____ a montar a caballo. (ir)

9. Él casi nunca _____ a sus parientes. (ver)

10. ¿A dónde _____ ustedes cuando los vi? (ir)

2.3 Uses of the preterite and the imperfect

The usage of the preterite and the imperfect indicates two different ways of looking at past events. The choice between the two forms depends on what type of events or actions are being described or conveyed. The preterite is used to describe a completed action or actions as well as the outcome of an action or actions. It refers to completed events that were repeated during a specific period of time or at one given point in time. The preterite is also used when reference is made as to when an action began, ended, or both. The imperfect ignores the outcome of an action and implies continuation of an action or actions. It also gives background information.

Example:

Cuando llamaste, estudiaba.
When you called, I was studying.

Exercises: Write the correct form of the preterite or the imperfect of the verbs in parentheses.

I. 1. Ellos me _____ ayer que _____ hablar con la profesora inmediatamente. (decir, necesitar)

2. Cuando yo _____ quince años _____ a esquiar. (tener, aprender)

3. De repente yo _____ lo que ellos _____. (comprender, querer)

4. Elena _____ dos veces la semana pasada en el Caribe. (bucear)

5. Todos los domingos mis hermanos _____ en casa de mis padres. (almorzar)

6. Anoche _____ a una discoteca con mi novia. (ir)

7. El domingo pasado yo _____ a unos turistas que _____ las vacaciones en México. (conocer, pasar)

8. Cuando tú me _____ , _____ música. (llamar, escuchar)

9. Nosotros _____ un paseo cuando _____ a llover. (dar, comenzar)

10. Ayer yo _____ fotos de los monumentos más importantes. (sacar)

Exercises: Complete the following paragraphs with the correct form of the preterite or the imperfect.

II. La semana pasada yo _____ (1, ir) a esquiar a unas montañas que están cerca de casa. _____ (2, Hacer) frío y _____ (3, nevar) mucho. Allí me _____ (4, esperar) unos viejos amigos. Cuando _____ (5, llegar) _____ (6, descubrir) que había olvidado los esquís en casa.

III. Anoche cuando yo _____ (1, estudiar) de repente _____ (2, escuchar) un ruido muy grande en la calle. Lo primero que yo _____ (3, hacer) fue asomarme a la ventana. Entonces _____ (4, ver) que había habido un accidente. _____ (5, Decidir) llamar a la policía. _____ (6, Bajar) las escaleras y _____ (7, ir) a socorrer al hombre que

_____ (8, estar) en el coche. Me _____ (9, alegrar) al ver que el hombre que _____(10, manejar) el coche no _____ (11, estar) herido. Sólo _____ (12, estar) muy asustado.

2.4 The future tense

The future tense indicates a future action, and it is formed by adding the future endings to the infinitive.

infinitive	*future ending*
hablar	-é, -ás, -á, -emos, -éis, -án
comer	-é, -ás, -á, -emos, -éis, -án
vivir	-é, -ás, -á, -emos, -éis, -án

In Spanish a future action may also be expressed by using *ir a* + infinitive and by using the present tense with reference to a future time.

Examples:

Llegaremos a Guatemala a la una de la tarde.
We will arrive in Guatemala at one o'clock in the afternoon.

Voy a comer en el restaurante.
I am going to eat in the restaurant.

Mañana como en el restaurante.
Tomorrow I will eat in the restaurant.

Exercises: Write the appropriate form of the future tense of the verbs in parentheses.

1. Ella _____ el apartamento la semana que viene. (alquilar)

2. Los invitados _____ al banquete a las ocho de la noche. (llegar)

3. Ustedes _____ cursos intensivos de español en México. (tomar)

4. Tú _____ a visitar a tus padres en la primavera. (ir)

5. Vosotros _____ en una isla pequeña del Pacífico. (aterrizar)

6. Yo _____ el artículo para el periódico la próxima semana. (escribir)

7. Desde mañana Ud. _____ sus horas laborales. (reducir)

8. Él _____ hacer lo que tiene que hacer. (prometer)

9. Nosotros no los _____ cuando vengan. (ver)

10. Ella _____ dentro de dos semanas. (volver)

2.4.1 The future tense of verbs with irregular stems

The future of irregular verbs is formed by adding the future endings to the irregular stems.

infinitive	future stem	future ending
decir	dir-	
haber	habr-	
hacer	har-	
poder	podr-	-é
poner	pondr-	-ás
querer	querr- +	-á
saber	sabr-	-emos
salir	saldr-	-éis
tener	tendr-	-án
valer	valdr-	
venir	vendr-	

Exercises: Write the appropriate form of the future tense of the verbs in parentheses.

1. Para mañana _____ que leer *Don Quijote*. (haber)

2. Los abogados _____ a última hora como siempre. (venir)

3. Nosotros _____ ir si tú nos envías las invitaciones. (poder)

4. Tú _____ asistir al festival de cine de San Sebastián. (querer)

5. Vosotros _____ sólo lo que sea necesario. (decir)

6. Usted _____ la información en el periódico. (poner)

7. Ella _____ todo lo posible para llegar a ser médico. (hacer)

8. La casa _____ más cada día que pase. (valer)

9. El avión para La Habana _____ a las tres de la madrugada. (salir)

10. Yo_____ el resultado de las elecciones por teléfono. (saber)

11. Roberto y Andrés _____ que despertarse temprano si no quieren perder el tren. (tener)

2.4.2 The future to express probability

The future tense is used in Spanish to express probability or wonder with regard to the present. The equivalent expressions in English are *probably*, *do you suppose*, *can . . . be*, etc.

Examples:

¿Dónde estará Alberto?
I wonder where Alberto is.

Estará en casa.
He is probably at home.

¿Qué hora será?
I wonder what time it is.

¿Será verdad?
Can it be true?

Exercises: Translate into Spanish the following sentences:

1. Do you suppose he remembers me?

   _____

2. I wonder where Roberto is.

   _____

3. What can he be thinking about?

   _____

4. He is probably busy as usual.

   _____

5. There are probably some advantages.

   _____

6. Where can my book be?

   _____

7. Gustavo must be playing with his friends.

   _____

8. Who can be calling at this time?

   _____

✓ Check Yourself

2.1 (The preterite)

1. habló 2. comí 3. pelearon 4. exigiste 5. recibimos 6. salió 7. barrieron 8. escribisteis
9. empezaron 10. creyó 11. oyeron

2.1.1 (Irregular preterites)

1. estuve 2. anduvo 3. tuvo 4. trajeron 5. pusieron 6. pudiste 7. quisimos 8. Hubo 9. fuisteis
10. produjo 11. dijeron 12. vino 13. fue

2.1.2 (Preterite of *-ir* stem-changing verbs)

1. murió 2. durmieron 3. seguí 4. prefirió 5. conseguimos 6. prefirieron 7. pidieron 8. dormí
9. siguieron 10. pedisteis

2.2.1 (The imperfect)

1. discutían 2. conducía 3. visitaban 4. viajaba 5. esquiaban 6. asistía 7. levantabas 8. organizabais
9. contaba 10. platicaba 11. estaba 12. tenía 13. deprimía 14. bailaban 15. gastaban, viajaban

2.2.2 (Irregular imperfect)

1. era 2. íbamos 3. veía 4. éramos 5. veían, eran 6. eras, eras 7. vivía, era 8. iba 9. veía 10. iban

2.3 (Uses of the preterite and the imperfect)

I. 1. dijeron, necesitaban 2. tenía, aprendí 3. comprendí, querían 4. buceó 5. almorzaban 6. fui
7. conocí, pasaban 8. llamaste, escuchaba 9. dábamos, comenzó 10. saqué

II. 1. fui 2. Hacía 3. nevaba 4. esperaban 5. llegué 6. descubrí

III. 1. estudiaba 2. escuché 3. hice 4. vi 5. Decidí 6. Bajé 7. fui 8. estaba 9. alegré 10. manejaba
11. estaba 12. estaba

2.4 (The future tense)

1. alquilará 2. llegarán 3. tomarán 4. irás 5. aterrizaréis 6. escribiré 7. reducirá 8. prometerá
9. veremos 10. volverá

2.4.1 (The future tense of verbs with irregular stems)

1. habrá 2. vendrán 3. podremos 4. querrás 5. diréis 6. pondrá 7. hará 8. valdrá 9. saldrá 10. sabré
11. tendrán

2.4.2 (The future to express probability)

1. ¿Se acordará de mí? 2. ¿Dónde estará Roberto? 3. ¿En qué pensará?/¿En qué estará pensando?
4. Estará ocupado como de costumbre. 5. Habrá algunas ventajas. 6. ¿Dónde estará mi libro?
7. Gustavo estará jugando con sus amigos. 8. ¿Quién llamará a estas horas?

Grade Yourself

Circle the numbers of the questions you missed, then fill in the total incorrect for each topic. If you answered more than three questions incorrectly, you need to focus on that topic. (If a topic has less than three questions and you had at least one wrong, we suggest you study that topic also. Read your textbook, a review book, or ask your teacher for help.)

Subject: The Indicative Mood: The Past and Future Tenses

Topic	Question Numbers	Number Incorrect
The preterite	**2.1:** 1, 2, 3, 4, 5, 6, 7, 8, 9, 10, 11	
Irregular preterites	**2.1.1:** 1, 2, 3, 4, 5, 6, 7, 8, 9, 10, 11, 12, 13	
Preterite of *-ir* stem-changing verbs	**2.1.2:** 1, 2, 3, 4, 5, 6, 7, 8, 9, 10	
The imperfect	**2.2.1:** 1, 2, 3, 4, 5, 6, 7, 8, 9, 10, 11, 12, 13, 14, 15	
Irregular imperfect	**2.2.2:** 1, 2, 3, 4, 5, 6, 7, 8, 9, 10	
Uses of the preterite and the imperfect	**2.3: I.** 1, 2, 3, 4, 5, 6, 7, 8, 9, 10 **II.** 1, 2, 3, 4, 5, 6 **III.** 1, 2, 3, 4, 5, 6, 7, 8, 9, 10, 11, 12	
The future tense	**2.4:** 1, 2, 3, 4, 5, 6, 7, 8, 9, 10	
The future tense of verbs with irregular stems	**2.4.1:** 1, 2, 3, 4, 5, 6, 7, 8, 9, 10, 11	
The future to express probability	**2.4.2:** 1, 2, 3, 4, 5, 6, 7, 8	

The Indicative Mood: The Compound Tenses

3

Brief Yourself

The progressive tenses express ongoing actions in the present, past, or future. The perfect tenses are used to focus on the completion of an action in relation to a moment in the present, past, or future.

Test Yourself

3.1 The present participle

The present participles of regular verbs are formed by adding *-ando* to the stem of *-ar* verbs, and *-iendo* to *-er* and *-ir* verbs.

hablar/habl*ando*
comer/com*iendo*
vivir/viv*iendo*

a) *-ir* stem-changing verbs change from *e* to *i* or *o* to *u*.

pedir/p*i*diendo sentir/s*i*ntiendo dormir/d*u*rmiendo

b) verbs whose stems end in a vowel change their endings from *-iendo* to *-yendo*.

creer/creyendo oír/oyendo   leer/leyendo

c) other irregular present participles:

decir/diciendo venir/viniendo   ir/yendo

Exercises: Indicate the present participle of the following verbs:

1. ser   _____

2. cerrar   _____

3. jugar   _____

4. creer   _____

5. seguir   _____

6. hacer   _____

7. oír   _____

8. leer   _____

9. construir _____

10. aprender   _____

11. defender   _____

12. decir   _____

13. conducir   _____

14. dormir   _____

15. servir _____

16. poner _____

17. ver _____

18. morir _____

19. ir _____

20. venir _____

3.2 The present progressive

The present progressive is formed with the present of *estar* plus the present participle. It is used to express ongoing actions in the present.

estoy		
estás		
está		hablando
estamos	+	comiendo
estáis		viviendo
están		

Examples:

Estás hablando demasiado.
You are talking too much.

Estoy comiendo muy poco últimamente.
I am eating very little lately.

Estamos viviendo muy cerca de todo.
We are living very close to everything.

Exercises: Fill in the blanks with the present progressive form of the verbs in parentheses.

1. Mi marido_____ un libro. (escribir)

2. Vosotros _____ un problema muy polémico. (discutir)

3. Ustedes _____ un tango. (bailar)

4. La cantante _____ un bolero. (cantar)

5. Yo _____ demasiado. (comer)

6. Ellas _____ en el banco. (trabajar)

7. La niña _____ con sus primas. (jugar)

8. Vosotros _____ una película de terror. (mirar)

9. El artista _____ un cuadro. (pintar)

10. Los perros _____ . (ladrar)

11. Todos _____ el árbol de Navidad. (decorar)

12. Los estudiantes _____ a conjugar los verbos. (aprender)

13. Él _____ el papel que perdió. (buscar)

14. Ella _____ la siesta. (dormir)

15. Mi abuelo _____ el periódico. (leer)

16. La madre _____ a sus hijos. (vestir)

17. El camarero ya _____ el postre. (traer)

18. El enfermo _____ de cáncer. (morir)

19. Tú _____ mucho dinero. (pedir)

20. Las patatas _____ . (hervir)

21. La policía _____ al borracho. (seguir)

22. La maestra _____ los ejercicios. (corregir)

23. El cocinero _____ el pollo. (freír)

24. Los fieles _____ misa en este momento. (oír)

25. Yo te _____ lo que tienes que hacer. (decir)

26. Los refugiados _____ de la violencia en su país. (huir)

3.3 The past progressive

The past progressive is formed with the imperfect or the preterite of *estar* and the present participle. It refers to an ongoing action in the past.

estaba/estuve

estabas/estuviste

estaba/estuvo

estábamos/estuvimos   +   hablando

estabais/estuvisteis

estaban/estuvieron

Example:

Estaba hablando en el pasillo.
I was talking in the hallway.

Exercises: Complete the sentences with the past progressive of the verbs in parentheses.

1. Cuando pasaste a recogerme, yo _____. (trabajar)

2. Yo _____ todo lo que necesitaba. (comprar)

3. Mis amigos_____ cuando llegué. (comer)

4. Tú _____ sin parar toda una hora. (hablar)

5. Ellas _____ la radio y tomando el sol. (escuchar)

6. El mecánico _____ su coche. (arreglar)

7. Nosotros _____ una casa o un apartamento amplio. (buscar)

8. Los muchachos _____ sus ejercicios antes de dormir. (hacer)

9. Vosotros _____ cuando el jefe entró. (discutir)

10. Los moros y los cristianos _____ durante siglos. (combatir)

11. Su esposo _____ mientras ella trabajaba. (dormir)

3.4 The future progressive

The future progressive is formed with the future of *estar* and the present participle. It is used to express an ongoing action in the future.

estaré

estarás

estará

estaremos   +   hablando

estaréis

estarán

Examples:

Estaremos hablando toda la noche.
We will be speaking all night.

Estaré comiendo a las diez.
I will be eating at ten.

Exercises: Fill in the blanks with the future progressive of the verb in parentheses.

1. Mañana a esta hora _____ a Santo Domingo. (volar)

2. En otoño los estudiantes _____ otra vez. (estudiar)

3. Este verano vosotros _____ y yo _____. (trabajar, descansar)

4. En un año los atletas _____ en los juegos olímpicos. (correr)

5. La fábrica _____ más de lo que podrá vender. (producir)

6. En cinco meses nosotros nos _____ las ganancias. (repartir)

7. En dos semanas, tú te _____ para tu boda. (preparar)

8. Pronto ellos _____ otra casa para vender. (construir)

9. La próxima semana, ellos _____ su quinto aniversario. (celebrar)

10. Cuando lleguen sus amistades, nosotros _____. (comer)

3.5 The past participle

Past participles of regular verbs are formed by adding -*ado* to the stem of -*ar* verbs, and -*ido* to -*er* and -*ir* verbs. The past participle, when used as a verb, always ends in an *o*, and there is no agreement of gender and number.

hablar/habl*ado*   comer/com*ido*   vivir/viv*ido*

Irregular past participles end in either -*to* or -*cho*.

abrir/abierto   cubrir/cubierto   hacer/hecho
decir/dicho   morir/muerto   escribir/escrito
bendecir/bendito   poner/puesto   romper/roto

volver/vuelto   freír /frito   resolver/ resuelto
ver/visto   satisfacer/satisfecho

Exercises: Indicate the past participle of the following verbs:

1. cubrir _____

2. decir _____

3. morir _____

4. abrir _____

5. escribir _____

6. resolver _____

7. volver _____

8. hacer _____

9. poner _____

10. romper _____

11. ver _____

12. satisfacer _____

13. llamar _____

14. caer _____

15. tener _____

16. pensar _____

17. indicar _____

18. freír _____

19. bendecir _____

3.6 The present perfect

The present perfect is formed with the present indicative of the auxiliary verb *haber* and the past participle. The present perfect is used to refer to completed actions initiated in the past in relation to the present.

he		
has		
ha		
hemos	+	hablado
habéis		
han		

Examples:

Yo he hablado con todos.
I have spoken with everybody.

¿Has comido en casa?
Have you eaten at home?

Exercises: Fill in the blank with the translation of the verbs in parentheses.

1. Nosotros _____ muchas felicitaciones esta Navidad. (have received)

2. Yo _____ a clase todos los días. (have gone)

3. Tú _____ todo el año en la cafetería. (have eaten)

4. Ustedes _____ tarde a clase muchas veces. (have arrived)

5. Nosotras ya _____ a una nueva direct ora. (have chosen)

6. Mi amigo y yo _____ la relación. (have broken)

7. Tú _____ mucha literatura latinoamericana. (have read)

8. Ellos _____ el trabajo en muy poco tiempo. (have written)

9. Yo no _____ al Museo de Antropología de México. (have returned)

10. Vosotras _____ una cena muy rica. (have prepared)

3.7 The pluperfect

The pluperfect is formed with the imperfect indicative of the auxiliary verb *haber* and the past participle. It is used to refer to an action prior to another action in the past.

había		
habías		
había		
habíamos	+	hablado
habíais		
habían		

Examples:

Ya habían hablado ruso antes de ir a Moscú.
They had spoken Russian before going to Moscow.

¿Habías comido antes en un restaurante gallego?
Had you eaten in a Galician restaurant before?

Ya habíamos vivido antes en esa ciudad.
We had already lived in that city.

Exercises: Fill in the blank with the translation of the words in parentheses.

1. Ya _____ cuando llamaron a la puerta. (we had eaten)

2. Hace algunos años él _____ sus estudios. (had finished)

3. Nosotros _____ esa novela antes. (had read)

4. La clase ya _____ cuando llegué. (it had started)

5. El año anterior ellos todavía no _____ a Costa Rica. (had not gone)

6. Él ya se _____ cuando lo llamaron. (had prepared)

7. Yo _____ antes con ese profesor. (had studied)

8. Te _____ en la última reunión. (had met)

9. Todavía no me_____ cuando sonó el despertador. (I had not awakened)

10. Ellos _____ por España antes. (had traveled)

11. Pensaba que tú todavía no _____ el trabajo para la clase. (had not written)

12. Dijeron que él ya se _____ antes de los mismos problemas. (had complained)

13. Ya _____ antes a este restaurante. (we had come)

3.8 The future perfect

The future perfect is formed with the future of the auxiliary verb *haber* and the past participle of the main verb. The future perfect is used to refer to future actions that will have been completed by a specific time in the future. It is also used to express probability of completed actions in the past.

habré

habrás

habrá

habremos   +   hablado

habréis

habrán

Examples:

Para las cuatro Juan ya habrá limpiado su casa.

By four o'clock, Juan will have already cleaned his house.

María tenía ganas de ver a su familia y habrá regresado a verla.

Maria felt like seeing her family and probably returned to see them.

Exercises: Complete the sentences with the future perfect of the verbs in parentheses.

1. Yo ya _____ la tarea para el lunes. (acabar)

2. Julio tenía una cita y se _____. (ir)

3. Nosotras ya _____ de empaquetar antes de las cuatro. (terminar)

4. Ellas _____ el problema cuando él llegue. (resolver)

5. Tú _____ mucho dinero antes de Navidad. (ahorrar)

6. Yo _____ todos los regalos antes de visitar a mi familia. (comprar)

7. Supongo que Uds. _____ los detalles antes de firmar el contrato. (aclarar)

8. Nuestras amigas _____ a casa antes de acabarse la fiesta. (regresar)

9. Elena se le olvidó su chequera y _____ a casa para recogerla. (volver)

10. No vamos a buscarla porque ella ya _____ a un taxi. (llamar)

3.9   The perfect progressive tenses

The perfect progressive tenses are used to express the completion of ongoing actions in relation to another present, past, or future moment.

a) The present perfect progressive is formed with the present perfect of *estar* plus the present participle of the main verb. It is used to express the completion of ongoing actions in relation to the present.

he		
has		
ha		
hemos	+	estado hablando
habéis		
han		

Examples:

He estado viviendo mucho tiempo con mis padres.
I have been living with my parents for a long time.

¿Han estado comiendo en la cafetería?
Have they been eating in the cafeteria?

b) The pluperfect progressive is formed with the pluperfect of *estar* plus the present participle of the main verb. It is used to express the completion of ongoing actions *in relation to a past moment.*

había		
habías		
había		
habíamos	+	estado hablando
habíais		
habían		

Examples:

Habíamos estado hablando demasiado.
We had been speaking too much.

Había estado viviendo por muchos años en el mismo apartamento.
He had been living for many years in the same apartment.

c) The future perfect progressive is formed with the future perfect of *estar* plus the present participle of the main verb. It is used to express the completion of ongoing actions in relation to some time in the future.

habré		
habrás		
habrá		
habremos	+	estado hablando
habréis		
habrán		

Examples:

Para las dos ya habrás estado comiendo.
By two you will have been eating already.

Para fin de año ya habrán estado viviendo en la Argentina.
By New Year's Eve they will have been already living in Argentina.

Exercises: Translate the verbs in parentheses using the appropriate perfect progressive tense.

1. Tú _____ por muchas horas. (have been talking)

2. Antes de comprar un coche, ellas _____ el autobús cada día. (had been taking)

3. Yo _____ todo el día. (have been studying)

4. Antes de enfermarme, yo _____ en la lluvia. (had been walking)

5. Ellos no _____ lo que debían. (have not been doing)

6. Nosotros _____ buenos comentarios sobre ti. (have been listening to)

7. Usted _____ por nada. (have been struggling)

8. Yo _____ una novela. (have been writing)

9. Él _____ el pollo. (has been cooking)

10. Tú _____ demasiado. (have been gossiping)

11. Mi suegra _____ todo otra vez. (has been observing)

12. Ellos se _____ para la carrera. (have been preparing)

13. Para cuando tú llegues, yo ya _____ por algunas horas. (will have been sleeping)

14. Cuando él venga, yo ya _____ en mi nuevo apartamento varios meses. (will have been living)

15. Para cuando su esposo decida dónde quiere ir, ella ya _____ las reservaciones para ir a Santo Domingo. (will have been making)

✓ Check Yourself

3.1   (The present participle)

1. siendo 2. cerrando 3. jugando 4. creyendo 5. siguiendo 6. haciendo 7. oyendo 8. leyendo
9. construyendo 10. aprendiendo 11. defendiendo 12. diciendo 13. conduciendo 14. durmiendo
15. sirviendo 16. poniendo 17. viendo 18. muriendo 19. yendo 20. viniendo

3.2   (The present progressive)

1. está escribiendo 2. estáis discutiendo 3. están bailando 4. está cantando 5. estoy comiendo 6. están
trabajando 7. está jugando 8. estáis mirando 9. está pintando 10. están ladrando 11. están decorando
12. están aprendiendo 13. está buscando 14. está durmiendo 15. está leyendo 16. está vistiendo
17. está trayendo 18. está muriendo 19. estás pidiendo 20. están hirviendo 21. está siguiendo 22. está
corrigiendo 23. está friendo 24. están oyendo 25. estoy diciendo 26. están huyendo

3.3   (The past progressive)

1. estaba trabajando 2. estaba/estuve comprando 3. estaban comiendo 4. estuviste hablando 5. estaban
escuchando 6. estaba arreglando 7. estábamos/estuvimos buscando 8. estuvieron haciendo 9. estabais
discutiendo 10. estuvieron combatiendo 11. estaba durmiendo

3.4   (The future progressive)

1. estaré volando 2. estarán estudiando 3. estaréis trabajando, estaré descansando 4. estarán corriendo
5. estará produciendo 6. estaremos repartiendo 7. estarás preparando 8. estarán construyendo
9. estarán celebrando 10. estaremos comiendo

3.5   (The past participle)

1. cubierto 2. dicho 3. muerto 4. abierto 5. escrito 6. resuelto 7. vuelto 8. hecho 9. puesto 10. roto
11. visto 12. satisfecho 13. llamado 14. caído 15. tenido 16. pensado 17. indicado 18. frito
19. bendito

3.6   (The present perfect)

1. hemos recibido 2. he ido 3. has comido 4. han llegado 5. hemos elegido 6. hemos roto 7. has leído
8. han escrito 9. he vuelto/he regresado 10. habéis preparado

3.7   (The pluperfect)

1. habíamos comido 2. había terminado 3. habíamos leído 4. había comenzado 5. habían ido 6. había preparado 7. había estudiado 8. había conocido 9. había despertado 10. habían viajado 11. habías escrito 12. había quejado 13. habíamos venido

3.8   (The future perfect)

1. habré acabado 2. habrá ido 3. habremos terminado 4. habrán resuelto 5. habrás ahorrado 6. habré comprado 7. habrán aclarado 8. habrán regresado 9. habrá vuelto 10. habrá llamado

3.9   (The perfect progressive tenses)

1. has estado hablando 2. habían estado tomando/cogiendo 3. he estado estudiando 4. había estado caminando/había estado andando 5. han estado haciendo 6. hemos estado escuchando 7. ha estado luchando 8. he estado escribiendo 9. ha estado cocinando 10. has estado chismeando 11. ha estado observando 12. han estado preparando 13. habré estado durmiendo 14. habré estado viviendo 15. habrá estado haciendo

Grade Yourself

Circle the numbers of the questions you missed, then fill in the total incorrect for each topic. If you answered more than three questions incorrectly, you need to focus on that topic. (If a topic has less than three questions and you had at least one wrong, we suggest you study that topic also. Read your textbook, a review book, or ask your teacher for help.)

Subject: The Indicative Mood: The Compound Tenses

Topic	Question Numbers	Number Incorrect
The present participle	**3.1:** 1, 2, 3, 4, 5, 6, 7, 8, 9, 10, 11, 12, 13, 14, 15, 16, 17, 18, 19, 20	
The present progressive	**3.2:** 1, 2, 3, 4, 5, 6, 7, 8, 9, 10, 11, 12, 13, 14, 15, 16, 17, 18, 19, 20, 21, 22, 23, 24, 25, 26	
The past progressive	**3.3:** 1, 2, 3, 4, 5, 6, 7, 8, 9, 10, 11	
The future progressive	**3.4:** 1, 2, 3, 4, 5, 6, 7, 8, 9, 10	
The past participle	**3.5:** 1, 2, 3, 4, 5, 6, 7, 8, 9, 10, 11, 12, 13, 14, 15, 16, 17, 18, 19	
The present perfect	**3.6:** 1, 2, 3, 4, 5, 6, 7, 8, 9, 10	
The pluperfect	**3.7:** 1, 2, 3, 4, 5, 6, 7, 8, 9, 10, 11, 12, 13	
The future perfect	**3.8:** 1, 2, 3, 4, 5, 6, 7, 8, 9, 10	
The perfect progressive tenses	**3.9:** 1, 2, 3, 4, 5, 6, 7, 8, 9, 10, 11, 12, 13, 14, 15	

The Conditional

4

Test Yourself

4.1 The conditional

The Spanish conditional has the English equivalent of *would* and it is formed by adding the conditional endings to the infinitive.

infinitive	conditional ending
hablar	+ -ía, -ías, -ía, -íamos, -íais, -ían
comer	+ -ía, -ías, -ía, -íamos, -íais, -ían
vivir	+ -ía, -ías, -ía, -íamos, -íais, -ían

Example:

Yo no vendería mi casa a ese precio.
I would not sell my house at that price.

Exercises: Complete the sentences with the appropriate forms of the conditional.

1. Ella también _____ feliz en esta ciudad. (ser)

2. ¿_____ ustedes ir conmigo a Bolivia o al Perú? (Preferir)

3. Él me dijo que me _____ el libro. (dar)

4. Ellos nunca _____ sobre la política de su país. (discutir)

5. Yo no _____ ese viejo autobús. (tomar)

6. Él insistió en que el no _____ eso a la fiesta. (llevar)

7. Ustedes se _____ muy a menudo en el supermercado. (ver)

8. A cualquiera le _____ lo mismo. (pasar)

9. Me imagino que en otra situación tú te _____ con Felipe. (casar)

10. Nosotros nunca le _____ su edad. (preguntar)

4.2 Irregular verbs in the conditional

The conditional of irregular verbs is formed by adding the conditional endings to the irregular stems.

infinitive	stem		conditional ending
decir	dir-		
haber	habr-		
hacer	har-		
poder	podr-		-ía
poner	pondr-		-ías
querer	querr-	+	-ía
saber	sabr-		-íamos
salir	saldr-		-íais
tener	tendr-		-ían
valer	valdr-		
venir	vendr-		

Example:

En esta ciudad los niños tendrían de todo.
In this city the children would have everything.

Exercises: Complete the sentences with the appropriate forms of the conditional.

1. Ellos _____ resolver el problema sin dificultad. (poder)

2. Sin mucho dinero Susana no _____ un viaje al extranjero. (hacer)

3. Nosotros _____ lo necesario antes de empezar el proyecto. (saber)

4. Tú _____ sin que nadie lo supiera. (salir)

5. Me imagino que ellos no _____ sin llamar primero. (venir)

6. Dijo que no _____ lecturas para el examen. (asignar)

7. Ese coche _____ aproximadamente unos $3.000. (valer)

8. Él lo dijo, pero yo nunca _____ eso. (decir)

9. En el nuevo trabajo ella _____ que levantarse temprano. (tener)

10. Ustedes se _____ furiosos con el frío que hace aquí. (poner)

11. ¿Qué _____ hacer tú? (querer)

4.3 Uses of the conditional

The conditional is used in Spanish as follows:

a) to express a future action with regard to the past.

Example:

Dijo que iría.
He said he would go.

b) to express probability in the past.

Example:

Serían las dos de la tarde cuando él llamó.
It was probably two o'clock in the afternoon when he called.

c) to express polite requests.

Example:

Me gustaría comprar el libro Como agua para chocolate, *por favor.*
I would like to buy the book *Like Water for Chocolate,* please.

d) to express what would happen if a condition is met.

Example:

En tu lugar, no saldría con Juan.
In your place, I would not go out with John.

e) when an *if*-clause expresses something contrary to fact. (See Part I, 6.6)

Example:

Si tuviera tiempo, iría a California.
If I had time, I would go to California.

Exercises: Complete the following sentences with the appropriate forms of the conditional.

1. ¿Qué hora _____ cuando llegó? (ser)

2. Dijeron que ellos _____ las puertas del museo a la diez de la mañana. (abrir)

3. ¿_____ usted decirme a qué hora sale el tren? (Poder)

4. Si yo fuera el gerente, él no me _____ que hiciera eso. (pedir)

5. En ese caso no _____ necesidad de cancelar la reunión. (haber)

6. Carmen _____ muy nerviosa si tuviera otra entrevista. (estar)

7. ¿Quién _____ a las dos de la mañana? (llamar)

8. Nosotros dijimos que _____ el trabajo. (hacer)

9. ¿_____ ustedes conmigo? No, no _____ contigo. (Salir, salir)

10. ¿Qué _____ si heredaras un millón de dólares? (comprar)

4.4 The conditional perfect

The conditional perfect is used to state what would have happened and it is formed with the conditional of *haber* + the past participle. The conditional perfect has the following usages:

a) to imply that which should have happened but did not happen. This may be expressed by a *si*-clause, which is usually in the pluperfect subjunctive (see Part I, 6.6), or by a *pero*-clause in the appropriate tense of the *indicative*.

Examples:

La comida habría sido mejor si no tuviera tanta sal.
The meal would have been better if it didn't have so much salt.

Carmen habría comprado el auto, pero sus padres se opusieron.
Carmen would have bought the car, but her parents were against it.

b) to express the English equivalents of conjecture expressed by *could have*, *must have*, or *probably*.

Example:

¿Me habrían escrito?
Could they have written to me?

c) to express a future perfect idea when the verb in the main clause is in the past.

Example:

Ricardo dijo que Emilio ya habría salido.
Ricardo said that Emilio would have already gone out.

d) to describe what would have happened if certain conditions had been met. The pattern of contrary-to-fact clauses or *si*-clauses is as follows:

si-clause	main or result clause
pluperfect subjunctive	perfect conditional

Example:

Habríamos obtenido buenas notas en los exámenes, si hubiéramos estudiado.
We would have received good grades in the exams, if we had studied.

Exercises: Complete the following sentences with the Spanish equivalents.

1. _____ contigo, si no hubiera tenido que trabajar. (I would have gone out)

2. Si hubiera visitado tu ciudad, yo te _____. (I would have called)

3. En tu situación yo también _____ el trabajo. (I would have left)

4. No _____ así si fuera usted. (I would not have spoken)

5. ¿Qué _____ tú en mi lugar? (would you have done)

6. Ellas _____ a la playa con sus amigos, pero estaba lloviendo. (would have gone)

7. ¿Le _____ flores? (would they have sent)

8. Elena _____ por teléfono como de costumbre y por eso llegó tan tarde. (must have been talking)

9. Ella lo _____ en la mesa. (she had probably left it)

10. Nosotros _____ la invitación. (would have refused)

✓ Check Yourself

4.1   (The conditional)

1. sería 2. Preferirían 3. daría 4. discutirían 5. tomaría 6. llevaría 7. verían 8. pasaría 9. casarías
10. preguntaríamos

4.2   (Irregular verbs in the conditional)

1. podrían 2. haría 3. sabríamos 4. saldrías 5. vendrían 6. asignaría 7. valdría 8. diría 9. tendría
10. pondrían 11. querrías

4.3   (Uses of the conditional)

1. sería 2. abrirían 3. Podría 4. pediría 5. habría 6. estaría 7. llamaría 8. haríamos 9. Saldrían,
saldríamos 10. comprarías

4.4   (The conditional perfect)

1. Habría salido 2. habría llamado 3. habría dejado 4. habría hablado 5. habrías hecho 6. habrían ido
7. habrían enviado/mandado 8. habría estado hablando 9. habría dejado 10. habríamos rechazado

Grade Yourself

Circle the numbers of the questions you missed, then fill in the total incorrect for each topic. If you answered more than three questions incorrectly, you need to focus on that topic. (If a topic has less than three questions and you had at least one wrong, we suggest you study that topic also. Read your textbook, a review book, or ask your teacher for help.)

Subject: The Conditional

Topic	Question Numbers	Number Incorrect
The conditional	**4.1:** 1, 2, 3, 4, 5, 6, 7, 8, 9, 10	
Irregular verbs in the conditional	**4.2:** 1, 2, 3, 4, 5, 6, 7, 8, 9, 10, 11	
Uses of the conditional	**4.3:** 1, 2, 3, 4, 5, 6, 7, 8, 9, 10	
The conditional perfect	**4.4:** 1, 2, 3, 4, 5, 6, 7, 8, 9, 10	

The Subjunctive Mood: Simple and Compound Tenses

5

Brief Yourself

Unlike the indicative mood, which is used to state facts or things that are clearly indicated, the subjunctive mood is used to express doubt, emotions, commands, suggestions, opinions, and subjective ideas. The subjunctive can be used in some independent clauses (after *tal vez, ojalá, quizás, probablemente,* etc.), as well as in dependent clauses.

Test Yourself

5.1 Present subjunctive of regular verbs

The present subjunctive of regular verbs is formed by substituting the present indicative endings with the present subjunctive endings. Note that the subjunctive endings use the opposite vowel (*-ar* verbs have an *e,* and *-er* and *-ir* verbs have an *a*).

-ar		*-er*		*-ir*	
habl-	e	com-	a	viv-	a
habl-	es	com-	as	viv-	as
habl-	e	com-	a	viv-	a
habl-	emos	com-	amos	viv-	amos
habl-	éis	com-	áis	viv-	áis
habl-	en	com-	an	viv-	an

Example:

Tal vez viva en Ecuador dentro de algunos.
I might live in Ecuador in a few years.

Exercises: Fill in the blanks with the present subjunctive of the verbs in parentheses.

1. Probablemente ellos _____ su lección para mañana. (terminar)

2. Quizás más tarde usted me _____ más atención. (prestar)

3. Tal vez _____ mucho tiempo antes de verte otra vez. (pasar)

4. Ojalá que nuestro equipo _____ el partido. (ganar)

5. Ella no quiere que nosotros _____ tan alto. (hablar)

6. Ojalá no _____ mañana. (llover)

7. No es sano que ustedes _____ tanto. (trabajar)

8. Es necesario que nosotros nos _____ los unos a los otros. (amar)

9. Es posible que tú _____ todo lo que ganas. (gastar)

10. Puede ser que vosotros _____ juntos el próximo año. (vivir)

5.1.1 Subjunctive of *-ar* and *-er* stem-changing verbs

-ar and *-er* stem-changing verbs have the same stem changes in the present subjunctive as they do in the present indicative. Note that *-ar* and *-er* stem-changing verbs do not have stem changes in the *nosotros* and *vosotros* forms. Some verbs that follow this pattern are *encontrar, querer, poder, volver, resolver, negar, soñar, sentar, acostar, costar, llover, nevar.*

e→ie	e→ie	o→ue	o→ue
pensar	*perder*	*volver*	*contar*
piense	pierda	vuelva	cuente
pienses	pierdas	vuelvas	cuentes
piense	pierda	vuelva	cuente
pensemos	perdamos	volvamos	contemos
penséis	perdáis	volváis	contéis
piensen	pierdan	vuelvan	cuenten

Example:

Ojalá pienses más en mí.
I hope you think more about me.

Exercises: Fill in the blanks with the the present subjunctive of the verbs in parentheses.

1. Ojalá que tú _____ lo que buscas. (encontrar)

2. No creo que ellos _____ estudiar más. (querer)

3. Espero que él _____ entenderlo. (poder)

4. Tal vez nosotros _____ al Caribe el próximo año. (volver)

5. Sin su ayuda no parece que se _____ los problemas. (resolver)

6. No conviene que ella _____ lo que pasó. (negar)

7. ¡Ojalá tú _____ con los angelitos! (soñar)

8. Nos prohíben que nosotros nos _____ en la hierba. (sentar)

9. Tus padres no quieren que te _____ tan tarde. (acostar)

10. Ojalá que la matrícula no _____ más el próximo año. (costar)

11. Quizás _____ o _____ mañana. (llover, nevar)

12. Seguiré apoyando a mi equipo aunque _____. (perder)

13. Conviene que tú _____ todo lo ocurrido. (contar)

5.1.2 Subjunctive of *-ir* stem-changing verbs

-ir stem-changing verbs follow the same stem changes as in the indicative. In addition, they have another stem change in the *nosotros* and *vosotros* forms. In these forms the *e* of the stem changes to *i*, and the *o* of the stem changes to *u*. Verbs that follow this pattern are *sentir, dormir, servir, pedir, preferir, mentir, repetir, vestir, divertirse.*

e→ie	o→ue	e→i
sentir	*dormir*	*servir*
sienta	duerma	sirva
sientas	duermas	sirvas
sienta	duerma	sirva
sintamos	durmamos	sirvamos
sintáis	durmáis	sirváis
sientan	duerman	sirvan

Example:

Quizás mañana sirvan la comida más temprano.
Tomorrow they might serve the food earlier.

Exercises: Fill in the blanks with the present subjunctive of the verbs in parentheses.

1. Ellos quizás _____ hacer algo diferente. (preferir)

2. Puede ser que todavía él nos _____ más dinero. (pedir)

3. A mi no me gusta que tú me _____. (mentir)

4. Siempre hay que decirle a él que _____ las preguntas en voz alta. (repetir)

5. No me importa cómo ella se_____. (vestir)

6. Lo importante es que uno se _____. (divertir)

7. No creo que en España las tiendas _____ los domingos. (cerrar)

8. Es conveniente que todos nosotros _____ ocho horas diarias. (dormir)

5.1.3 Verbs with irregularities in the first person singular indicative.

Verbs with irregularities in the first person singular indicative have the same irregularities in all forms of the subjunctive. Verbs that have a *g*, *y*, or *z* in the *yo* form have this irregularity in all the forms of the subjunctive. Verbs with a *g* in the subjunctive stem are *decir, venir, traer, hacer, oír, salir, valer, tener.* Verbs with a *y* in the subjunctive stem are *concluir, recluir, obstruir.* Verbs with a *z* in the subjunctive stem are *conocer, conducir, parecer, producir.*

present indicative

digo, pongo, vengo, concluyo, conozco

present subjunctive

diga, digas, diga, digamos, digáis, digan

ponga, pongas, ponga, pongamos, pongáis, pongan

venga, vengas, venga, vengamos, vengáis, vengan

concluya, concluyas, concluya, concluyamos, concluyáis, concluyan

conozca, conozcas, conozca, conozcamos, conozcáis, conozcan

Example:

Ojalá yo concluya rápido este ejercicio.
I hope I finish this exercise quickly.

Exercises: Fill in the blanks with the present subjunctive of the verbs in parentheses.

1. Mañana tal vez _____ nevando. (continuar)

2. Nos vamos cuando él _____. (decir)

3. Conviene que nosotros nos _____ todos los días. (reunir)

4. Probablemente los vecinos _____ nuestras conversaciones. (oír)

5. Puede ser que nosotros _____ que comprar más regalos. (tener)

6. Ojalá él lo _____ por correo. (enviar)

7. Aunque _____ increíble, ella es completamente bilingüe. (parecer)

8. No es aconsejable que alguien _____ borracho. (conducir)

9. Espero que cuando él _____ , _____ lo que le pedí. (venir, traer)

10. Probablemente no _____ más nieve este invierno. (caer)

11. No creo que este regalo _____ tanto. (valer)

12. Espero que mañana_____ buen tiempo. (hacer)

13. Tal vez él se _____ a dieta pronto. (poner)

14. Quizás el avión no _____ a tiempo. (salir)

15. Conviene que se _____ este ejercicio. (concluir)

5.1.4 Present subjunctive of *ir, ser, haber, dar, saber,* and *estar*

Ir, ser, haber, dar, saber, and *estar* are irregular in the present subjunctive. Note, however, that although the verb stems are irregular, these verbs do take the regular subjunctive endings.

ir: vaya, vayas, vaya, vayamos, vayáis, vayan

ser: sea, seas, sea, seamos, seáis, sean

haber: haya, hayas, haya, hayamos, hayáis, hayan

dar: dé, des, dé, demos, deis, den

saber: sepa, sepas, sepa, sepamos, sepáis, sepan

estar: esté, estés, esté, estemos, estéis, estén

Example:

Quizás haya más de una fiesta este viernes.
There might be more than one party this Friday.

Exercises: Fill in the blanks with the present subjunctive of the verbs in parentheses.

1. No creo que nosotros _____ todas las respuestas. (saber)

2. Alguien que _____ bilingüe tendrá más oportunidades de trabajo. (ser)

3. Ojalá ya no _____ más exámenes este semestre. (haber)

4. Probablemente nosotros_____ de viaje otra vez este verano. (ir)

5. Preferimos que los profesores nos _____ buenas notas. (dar)

6. Ojalá que el examen _____ fácil. (ser)

7. Tal vez el libro que necesito _____ en la biblioteca. (estar)

5.1.5 Verbs with orthographic changes

Verbs that end in *-gar, -gir, -guir, -car, -zar, -ger, -cer* have the following spelling changes in all forms of the present subjunctive:

g→gu	llegar:	llegue, llegues, llegue, lleguemos, lleguéis, lleguen
g→j	elegir:	elija, elijas, elija, elijamos, elijáis, elijan
gu→g	seguir:	siga, sigas, siga, sigamos, sigáis, sigan
c→qu	sacar:	saque, saques, saque, saquemos, saquéis, saquen
z→c	cruzar:	cruce, cruces, cruce, crucemos, crucéis, crucen
g→j	proteger:	proteja, protejas, proteja, protejamos, protejáis, protejan
c→z	vencer:	venza, venzas, venza, venzamos, venzáis, venzan

Example:

Espero que él llegue pronto.
I hope he arrives soon.

Exercises: Fill in the blanks with the present subjunctive of the verbs in parentheses.

1. Quizás la compañía _____ todos los gastos. (pagar)

2. Ojalá yo no _____ más resfriados. (coger)

3. Probablemente nosotros _____ otro apartamento. (buscar)

4. No creo que él _____ los diferentes acentos hispanos. (distinguir)

5. Conviene que ellos _____ claramente las correcciones. (marcar)

6. No creo que me _____ aunque siga insistiendo. (convencer)

7. Quizás el nuevo director _____ tan bien como el anterior. (dirigir)

8. Probablemente ella _____ las metas que se ha propuesto. (alcanzar)

9. Cuando ellos _____ nos llamarán. (llegar)

10. Dudo que esta crema de sol _____ mucho la piel. (proteger)

5.2 Imperfect subjunctive

The imperfect subjunctive of regular verbs is formed by substituting the *-ron* of the third person plural of the preterite with the appropriate imperfect subjunctive endings *-ra, -ras, -ra, -'ramos, -rais, -ran*.

habla*ra*	comie*ra*	vivie*ra*
habla*ras*	comie*ras*	vivie*ras*
habla*ra*	comie*ra*	vivie*ra*
hablá*ramos*	comié*ramos*	vivié*ramos*
habla*rais*	comie*rais*	vivie*rais*
habla*ran*	comie*ran*	vivie*ran*

Example:

Ojalá no hablaran tan alto.
I wish they did not speak so loud.

Exercises: Fill in the blanks with the imperfect subjunctive of the verbs in parentheses.

1. Me aconsejaron que _____ otra cuenta bancaria. (abrir)

2. Ojalá tú me _____ antes de tomar las decisiones. (consultar)

3. No querían que su amigo _____ tanto. (sufrir)

4. La vendedora esperaba que nosotros le _____ el lavaplatos. (comprar)

5. A mis padres les molestaba que yo les _____. (gritar)

5.2.1 Verbs that are irregular in the preterite indicative

Verbs that are irregular in the preterite indicative show the same irregularities in the imperfect subjunctive.

<u>preterite</u>

estuvieron, durmieron, fueron, pidieron

<u>imperfect subjunctive</u>

estar: estuviera, estuvieras, estuviera, estuviéramos, estuvierais, estuvieran

dormir: durmiera, durmieras, durmiera, durmiéramos, durmierais, durmieran

ser: fuera, fueras, fuera, fuéramos, fuerais, fueran

pedir: pidiera, pidieras, pidiera, pidiéramos, pidierais, pidieran

Example:

Me gustaría que estuvieras aquí conmigo.
I would like you to be here with me.

Exercises: Fill in the blanks with the imperfect subjunctive of the verbs in parentheses.

1. Me temía que ella no _____.
    (venir)

2. Ojalá ellos _____ dinero y no
    me lo _____ a mí. (tener, pedir)

3. Yo esperaba que ella le _____
    algo. (decir)

4. Era una lástima que Carlos no _____
    venir. (poder)

5. El autor quería que el público _____
    sus libros. (leer)

6. Nos recojimos antes de que _____
    el aguacero. (caer)

7. Fue una pena que nosotros nos
    _____ durante la charla. (dormir)

8. Mis amigos me decían que _____
    despacio. (conducir)

9. Bajamos el volumen de la música para que los
    vecinos no la _____. (oír)

10. Nos alegramos de que no _____
    heridos en el accidente. (haber)

11. Aunque mi carro _____ más
    espacio no creo que_____ todos
    ellos. (tener, caber)

12. Me fui antes de que _____ el
    concierto. (concluir)

5.3 Present and imperfect progressive of the subjunctive

The present and imperfect progressive are formed in the following manner:

a) with the present subjunctive of *estar* plus the present participle.

esté		
estés		
esté		
estemos	+	hablando
estéis	+	comiendo
estén	+	viviendo

b) with the imperfect of *estar* plus the past participle.

estuviera		
estuvieras		
estuviera	+	hablando
estuviéramos	+	comiendo
estuvierais	+	viviendo
estuvieran		

Example:

Tal vez ella todavía esté hablando por teléfono.
She might still be talking on the phone.

Exercises: Fill in the blanks with the progressive subjunctive according to the English translation.

1. Ojalá él _____ cuando
    hablábamos. (he was listening)

2. Tal vez ella _____ cuando
    la llamamos. (she was sleeping)

3. No me gusta que ellos siempre te
    _____. (are defending you)

4. No creo que se _____ de ti.
    (he is laughing at you)

5. Probablemente _____ todo lo
    que discutimos. (they are hearing)

6. Tal vez ella _____ en
    su cuarto. (is reading)

7. Quizás todavía elles _____ juntos. (are going out)

8. Si no _____, saldríamos. (if it weren't raining)

9. Cuando llegué, me molestó que ellos _____. (were crying)

10. No creo que _____ todo lo que deben. (they are doing)

5.4 Present perfect subjunctive

The present perfect subjunctive is formed with the present subjunctive of the auxiliary verb *haber* and the past participle of the main verb. It is the equivalent of the present perfect indicative, but in the subjunctive mood.

haya		
hayas		
haya	+	hablado
hayamos	+	comido
hayáis	+	vivido
hayan		

Example:

¿Crees que ya haya comido?
Do you think he has already eaten?

Exercises: Give the Spanish equivalent of the present perfect subjunctive of the verbs in parentheses.

1. Quizás él ya se _____. (has gone to bed)

2. Tal vez el profesor ya _____ el examen. (has prepared)

3. Puede ser que ella ya _____ la decisión. (has made)

4. Ojalá que mi amiga_____ la clase de geografía. (has taken)

5. ¿Cómo es posible que tú nos _____ todo este tiempo? (have lied)

6. Probablemente se _____ otra vez. (has fallen in love)

7. Es una pena que él _____ la ventana. (has broken)

8. Quizás ella me _____ un número de teléfono equivocado. (has given me)

9. Hasta ahora no creo que se _____ nadie. (has found out)

10. Puede ser que él _____ sin pedir permiso. (has gone)

5.4.1 Pluperfect subjunctive

The pluperfect subjunctive is formed with the imperfect subjunctive of the auxiliary verb *haber* and the past participle of the main verb. It is the equivalent of the pluperfect perfect indicative, but in the subjunctive mood.

hubiera		
hubieras		
hubiera	+	hablado
hubiéramos	+	comido
hubierais	+	vivido
hubieran		

Example:

Ojalá hubiera hablado antes del problema.
I wish I had spoken before about the problem.

Exercises: Give the Spanish equivalent of the pluperfect subjunctive of the verbs in parentheses.

1. Quería que ella_____ más comida a la fiesta. (had brought)

2. Tal vez él ya lo _____ antes. (had studied)

3. Sin estudiar, probablemente tú no
_____ una buena nota. (had gotten)

4. Puede ser que ella ya _____ en Guatemala antes. (had been)

5. Quizás otra clase no _____ tan aburrida. (would have been)

6. Estaría bien si todos nosotros _____ español desde pequeños. (had spoken)

7. Tal vez ella lo _____, pero ya es tarde. (had said it)

8. Sin dinero quizás no _____ sus estudios. (wouldn't have finished)

9. Con amigos en el país tal vez
_____ más fácil adaptarse. (would have been)

10. Puede ser que él _____ trabajo por su título. (had found)

5.4.2 Perfect progressive forms of the subjunctive

The perfect progressive forms of the subjunctive are the present perfect progressive and the pluperfect progressive.

a) The present perfect progressive is formed with the present perfect subjunctive of the auxiliary verb *haber* plus a present participle. It is used when the main verb is in the present and refers to a completed ongoing action in the past.

haya estado

hayas estado

haya estado

hayamos estado	+	hablando
hayáis estado	+	comiendo
hayan estado	+	viviendo

b) The pluperfect progressive is formed with the pluperfect subjunctive of the auxiliary verb *haber* plus a pre-

sent participle. It is used to refer to a completed ongoing action in a moment in the past prior to another past action.

hubiera estado

hubieras estado

hubiera estado

hubiéramos estado	+	hablando
hubierais estado	+	comiendo
hubieran estado	+	viviendo

Example:

Si no hubiéramos estado hablando, no estaríamos tan cansados.
If we hadn't been talking, we would not be so tired.

Exercises: Give the Spanish equivalent of the present perfect or pluperfect progressive of the subjunctive of the verbs in parentheses.

1. Quizás él no _____ lo que prometió. (has not been doing)

2. Ojalá yo no _____ cuando llamaste. (had not been eating)

3. Sin la última pelea, tal vez _____ todavía. (we would have still been going out)

4. Quizás Ana no _____ tanto como dice. (has not been suffering)

5. No parece que él _____ las lecturas para la clase. (has been reading)

6. Ojalá no _____ otra universidad cuando los conocí. (they had not been looking for)

7. Tal vez usted no _____ en lo que estaba diciendo. (you had not been thinking)

8. Si José_____ en el mismo sitio, nos habríamos quedado allí. (had been living)

9. Còn esa borrachera tal vez _____
   mucho ron. (has been drinking)

10. No creo que ella me _____ todo
    este tiempo. (has been deceiving me)

11. Si ellos nos _____,
    nosotros lo sabríamos. (had been lying)

5.5 Sequence of tenses

The choice of verb used in the dependent clause is influenced by the idea being expressed. The tense of the verb used in the main clause determines also the subjunctive tense used in the dependent clause. The normal sequence of tenses is as follows:

main clause	dependent clause
verb in indicative	verb in subjunctive
present	
present perfect	present subjunctive
future	present perfect subjunctive
commands	
preterite	
imperfect	imperfect subjunctive
pluperfect	pluperfect subjunctive
conditional	
conditional perfect	

Examples:

Yo prohíbo que ella salga.
I prohibit her to leave.

Tú has prohibido que ella salga.
You have prohibited her to leave.

Él prohibirá que ella salga.
He will prohibit her to leave.

¡Prohíba usted que ella salga!
Prohibit her to leave!

Ellos prohibieron que ella saliera.
They prohibited her to leave.

Tú prohibías que ella saliera.
You used to prohibit her to leave.

Yo prohibiría que ella saliera.
I would prohibit her to leave.

Ellos habían prohibido que ella saliera.
They had prohibited her to leave.

Tú habrías prohibido que ella saliera.
You would have prohibited her to leave.

The present indicative and the past subjunctive can be combined as necessary to express an action or idea that has already occurred, or to communicate the idea that the speaker wishes to express.

Example:

No me gusta que discutieras con ella.
I don't like that you argued with her.

Exercises: Complete the sentences with the Spanish translation of the verbs in parentheses.

1. No creo que él _____ a la fiesta. (will go)

2. Probablemente él _____ a la biblioteca. (went)

3. No parece que él _____ de vacaciones. (has gone)

4. No sabía que él _____ a comprar la comida. (had gone)

5. Le digo que _____ más para el examen. (to study)

6. Le han dicho que _____ más. (to read)

7. Le dije que _____ menos. (to drink)

8. Le había dicho que _____ con sus amigos. (to go out)

9. Es importante que ella _____ las reservaciones. (make)

10. Será importante que ellos _____ las recomendaciones. (follow)

11. Fue necesario que ella _____ peso. (lose)

12. Era escandaloso que él _____ tanto ruido. (made)

13. Me alegró que ellos _____ al teatro. (had gone)

14. Me enojó que ella no _____ a la reunión. (had come)

15. Me gustó que él _____. (had called)

16. Ellos me piden que _____ el pasaporte. (I take out)

17. Te llamaré tan pronto como _____. (I can)

18. Siempre había querido que ella _____ a la universidad. (go)

19. Dudaba que su tía _____ hoy. (had arrived)

20. Quiero que tú _____ al trabajo. (go)

21. Espero que ya _____ el contrato. (they have done)

22. Esperaban que _____ en su casa. (we would eat)

23. Sus padres han permitido que Rosita _____. (leave)

24. Querrán que nosotros _____ pronto. (finish)

25. Sugiera usted que ella _____ más temprano. (come)

✓ Check Yourself

5.1   **(Present subjunctive of regular verbs)**

1. terminen 2. preste 3. pase 4. gane 5. hablemos 6. llueva 7. trabajen 8. amemos 9. gastes 10. viváis

5.1.1   **(Subjunctive of *-ar* and *-er* stem-changing verbs)**

1. encuentres 2. quieran 3. pueda 4. volvamos 5. resuelvan 6. niegue 7. sueñes 8. sentemos 9. acuestes 10. cueste 11. llueva, nieve 12. pierda 13. cuentes

5.1.2   **(Subjunctive of *-ir* stem-changing verbs)**

1. prefieran 2. pida 3. mientas 4. repita 5. vista . divierta 7. cierren 8. durmamos

5.1.3   **(Verbs with irregularities in the first person singular indicative)**

1. continúe 2. diga 3. reunamos 4. oigan 5. tengamos 6. envíe 7. parezca 8. conduzca 9. venga, traiga 10. caiga 11. valga 12. haga 13. ponga 14. salga 15. concluya

5.1.4   **(Present subjunctive of *ir*, *ser*, *haber*, *dar*, *saber*, and *estar*)**

1. sepamos 2. sea 3. haya 4. vayamos 5. den 6. sea 7. esté

5.1.5   **(Verbs with orthographic changes)**

1. pague 2. coja 3. busquemos 4. distinga 5. marquen 6. convenza 7. dirija 8. alcance 9. lleguen 10. proteja

5.2   **(Imperfect subjunctive)**

1. abriera 2. consultaras 3. sufriera 4. compráramos 5. gritara

5.2.1   **(Verbs that are irregular in the preterite indicative)**

1. viniera 2. tuvieran, pidieran 3. dijera 4. pudiera 5. leyera 6. cayera 7. durmiéramos 8. condujera 9. oyeran 10. hubiera 11. tuviera, cupieran 12. concluyera

5.3   **(Present and imperfect progressive of the subjunctive)**

1. estuviera escuchando 2. estuviera durmiendo 3. estén defendiendo 4. esté riendo 5. estén oyendo 6. esté leyendo 7. estén saliendo 8. estuviera lloviendo 9. estuvieran llorando 10. estén haciendo

5.4   **(Present perfect subjunctive)**

1. haya acostado 2. haya preparado 3. haya hecho 4. haya tomado 5. hayas mentido 6. haya enamorado 7. haya roto 8. haya dado 9. haya enterado 10. haya ido

5.4.1   **(Pluperfect subjunctive)**

1. hubiera traído 2. hubiera estudiado 3. hubieras sacado 4. hubiera estado 5. hubiera sido 6. hubiéramos hablado 7. hubiera dicho 8. hubiera acabado 9. hubiera sido 10. hubiera encontrado

5.4.2   **(Perfect progressive forms of the subjunctive)**

1. haya estado haciendo 2. hubiera estado comiendo 3. hubiéramos estado saliendo 4. haya estado sufriendo 5. haya estado leyendo 6. hubieran estado buscando 7. hubiera estado pensando 8. hubiera estado viviendo 9. haya estado tomando/ bebiendo 10. haya estado engañando 11. hubieran estado mintiendo

5.5   **(Sequence of tenses)**

1. vaya 2. fuera 3. haya ido 4. hubiera ido 5. estudie 6. lea 7. bebiera 8. saliera 9. haga 10. sigan 11. perdiera 12. hiciera 13. hubieran ido 14. hubiera venido 15. hubiera llamado 16. saque 17. pueda 18. fuera 19. hubiera llegado 20. vayas 21. hayan hecho 22. comiéramos 23. salga 24. acabemos 25. venga

Grade Yourself

Circle the numbers of the questions you missed, then fill in the total incorrect for each topic. If you answered more than three questions incorrectly, you need to focus on that topic. (If a topic has less than three questions and you had at least one wrong, we suggest you study that topic also. Read your textbook, a review book, or ask your teacher for help.)

Subject: The Subjunctive Mood: Simple and Compound Tenses

Topic	Question Numbers	Number Incorrect
Present subjunctive of regular verbs	**5.1:** 1, 2, 3, 4, 5, 6, 7, 8, 9, 10	
Subjunctive of -ar and -er stem-changing verbs	**5.1.1:** 1, 2, 3, 4, 5, 6, 7, 8, 9, 10, 11, 12, 13	
Subjunctive of -ir stem-changing verbs	**5.1.2:** 1, 2, 3, 4, 5, 6, 7, 8	
Verbs with irregularities in the first person singular indicative	**5.1.3:** 1, 2, 3, 4, 5, 6, 7, 8, 9, 10, 11, 12, 13, 14, 15	
Present subjunctive of *ir, ser, haber, dar, saber,* and *estar*	**5.1.4:** 1, 2, 3, 4, 5, 6, 7	
Verbs with orthographic changes	**5.1.5:** 1, 2, 3, 4, 5, 6, 7, 8, 9, 10	
Imperfect subjunctive	**5.2:** 1, 2, 3, 4, 5	
Verbs that are irregular in the preterite indicative	**5.2.1:** 1, 2, 3, 4, 5, 6, 7, 8, 9, 10, 11, 12	
Present and imperfect progressive of the subjunctive	**5.3:** 1, 2, 3, 4, 5, 6, 7, 8, 9, 10	
Present perfect subjunctive	**5.4:** 1, 2, 3, 4, 5, 6, 7, 8, 9, 10	
Pluperfect subjunctive	**5.4.1:** 1, 2, 3, 4, 5, 6, 7, 8, 9, 10	
Perfect progressive forms of the subjunctive	**5.4.2:** 1, 2, 3, 4, 5, 6, 7, 8, 9, 10, 11	
Sequence of tenses	**5.5:** 1, 2, 3, 4, 5, 6, 7, 8, 9, 10, 11, 12, 13, 14, 15, 16, 17, 18, 19, 20, 21, 22, 23, 24, 25	

Uses of the Subjunctive

Brief Yourself

The subjunctive mood is used to present ideas that are not facts. It conveys concepts that are hypothetical, contrary to fact, and/or embody feelings, judgments, and emotions of the speaker toward a state or action.

Test Yourself

6.1 The subjunctive in dependent clauses

The subjunctive usually appears in the dependent clause of a complex sentence. The dependent clause is usually classified as a noun clause, an adjective clause, or an adverbial clause.

6.2 The subjunctive in noun clauses

Dependent clauses are classified as noun clauses when they function as a noun. The subjunctive is used in noun clauses after *que* when the dependent and independent clauses have two different subjects and the verb in the main clause expresses wish, desire, command, preference, approval, advice, permission, prohibition, or suggestion. It is also used in the dependent clause after verbs that express doubt, denial, uncertainty, emotion, feeling, and hope. If the dependent and independent clauses have the same subject, the infinitive is used.

Examples:

Pedro quiere   *que*   *Juan lea el periódico todos los días.*
(independent clause)   (dependent clause)

Pedro wants Juan to read the newspaper every day.

Juan quiere leer el periódico todos los días.
Juan wants to read the newspaper every day.

6.2.1 The subjunctive after verbs of emotion, feeling, and hope

The subjunctive is used in the dependent clause introduced by *que* when verbs and phrases that express emotion, feeling, and hope appear in the independent clause. The dependent and independent clauses must have different subjects. Some commonly used verbs and expressions are:

alegrarse de que	to be happy that
estar encantado de que	to be delighted that
(me) gusta que	I like that
(me) pone contento que	it makes me happy that
(me) hace feliz que	it makes me happy that
(me) encanta que	I am delighted that
(me) enoja que	it makes me angry that
(me) irrita que	it irritates me that
(me) molesta que	it bothers me that
(me) enfada que	it angers me that
(me) desilusiona	it disappoints me that
(me) entristece que	it saddens me that
sentir que	to be sorry that
lamentar que	to regret that

(me) sorprende que	it surprises me that
(me) emociona que	it thrills me that
(me) conmueve que	it moves me that
enorgullecerse de que	to take pride that
temer que	to fear that
tener miedo de que	to fear that
esperar que	to hope that
desear que	to wish that

Example:

Me sorprende que usted no pueda ir con su familia.
It surprises me that you cannot go with your family.

Exercises: Write the correct form of the subjunctive or the infinitive of the verbs in parentheses. Pay attention to the verb tenses.

1. Me alegro que tú _____ con nosotros. (venir)

2. Me conmovió que ellos me _____ un reloj. (regalar)

3. Temen que la información que les di _____ equivocada. (estar)

4. Les gusta que Pedro _____ en las fiestas. (cantar)

5. Me pone contento _____ que tú fuiste a España. (saber)

6. Nos entristece que _____ tanta gente pobre. (haber)

7. Esperaba que Enrique _____ a buscarme. (pasar)

8. Me irrita que ella _____ tan insistente. (ser)

9. Se enorgullecieron de que su hijo _____ el primer puesto de su clase. (recibir)

10. Me enoja que ellos _____ que esperar tanto. (tener)

11. Espero que tú _____ llegar sin ningún problema. (poder)

12. La madre deseaba que Carlota _____ con su novio. (romper)

6.2.2 The subjunctive after verbs of volition

The subjunctive is used after verbs or expressions that indicate wish, desire, order, suggestion, demand, request, prohibition, or permission of an action. Some commonly used verbs and expressions are:

aprobar	to approve
aconsejar	to advise
suplicar	to beg
dejar	to allow
desear	to desire
empeñarse en	to insist
gustar	to please
hacer	to make
impedir	to prevent
insistir	to insist
pedir	to ask
permitir	to permit
proponer	to propose
rogar	to beg
prohibir	to prohibit
sugerir	to suggest
mandar	to order
decir	to tell, to order, to command

Example:

Le permitió que saliera con sus amigos.
He allowed her to go out with her friends.

The indirect object pronouns are often used with the following verbs: *aconsejar, mandar, pedir, permitir, prohibir, recomendar, rogar, sugerir,* and *suplicar.*

Example:

Le pido a Cristina que apague la luz.
I ask Cristina to turn off the light.

Exercises: Complete the sentences with the correct form of the subjunctive or the infinitive. Be careful with the sequence of tenses.

1. Ellos aprueban que ustedes _____ a la reunión del consorcio. (ir)

2. Carlos le aconsejó a Teresa que _____ dinero. (ahorrar)

3. Tú te empeñas en que Josefina _____ al enfermo en el hospital. (visitar)

4. Los estudiantes desean que los profesores _____ más vacaciones. (tener)

5. Yo prefiero _____ una película dramática. (ver)

6. A ti te gusta _____ cuentos infantiles. (escribir)

7. Le había dicho que _____ para el examen de matemáticas. (estudiar)

8. Todos dudaban que él _____ la dirección correcta. (saber)

9. Vosotras impedís que ellas _____ la dirección de Alejandro. (obtener)

10. Nosotros le queremos _____ el regalo. (dar)

11. El padre le prohíbe al niño que se _____ en la piscina. (bañar)

6.2.3 The subjunctive after verbs of uncertainty, doubt, or denial

The subjunctive is used after verbs or expressions that indicate doubt, uncertainty, or disbelief with regard to emotions, actions, or events. The subjunctive is used in the dependent clause when the following verbs or expressions appear in the independent clause, provided that the two clauses have different subjects:

dudar	to doubt
negar	to deny
no creer que	not to believe that
no decir que	not to say that
no es verdad	it is not true
no estar seguro	not to be sure
no opinar que	not to believe that
no saber que	not to know that
pensar que	not to think that

When doubt is not conveyed, the indicative is used. Some verbs and expressions that take the indicative are:

no dudar	does not doubt
no negar	does not deny
creer	to believe
decir que	to say that
es verdad que	it is true that
estar seguro	to be sure

Examples:

No creo que él sepa que tiene que llegar a las nueve de la noche.
I doubt that he knows that he should arrive at nine o'clock P.M.

Creo que él sabe que tiene que llegar a las nueve de la noche.
I think that he knows that must arrive at nine o'clock P.M.

The above-mentioned verbs and expressions, when used in interrogative sentences, may take the subjunctive or the indicative, depending on the message that is being conveyed by the speaker.

Examples:

¿Crees que el chico es muy inteligente?
Do you think the boy is very intelligent? (I believe so.)

¿Crees que el chico sea muy inteligente?
Do you believe that the boy is very intelligent? (I don't know, or, I don't think so.)

Uncertainty is also implied by *por ... que*.

Example:

Por buenos que sean los músicos, no irán al concierto.
However good the musicians may be, they will not go to the concert.

Exercises: Complete the following sentences with the appropriate form of the subjunctive or the indicative. Be careful with the sequence of tenses.

1. Dudo que ellos _____ razón. (tener)

2. No dudé que ellos _____ tener tres meses de vacaciones. (poder)

3. Creíste todo lo que ellos te _____. (decir)

4. Es verdad que ella _____ a mi familia. (conocer)

5. Están seguros que ellos _____ las llaves en mi casa ayer. (dejar)

6. Dicen que ustedes no _____ por su cuenta. (ir)

7. ¿Piensas que sus padres _____ muy ricos? (ser) [I think so.]

8. Pensamos que ustedes _____ medicina. (estudiar)

9. Sé que usted _____ danés. (hablar)

10. Deseo que las crisis internacionales _____ rápidamente. (mejorar)

6.2.4 The subjunctive with impersonal expressions

Impersonal expressions, except those indicating certainty, are followed by the subjunctive if the dependent verb has a specific subject introduced by *que*. If this is not the case, the infinitive is used. The following is a partial list of commonly used impersonal expressions that take the subjunctive whenever a specific subject is implied:

es necesario	it is necessary
es posible	it is possible
es preciso	it is necessary
es imposible	it is impossible
es importante	it is important
es probable	it is probable
es (una) lástima	it is a pity
es improbable	it is improbable
es triste	it is sad
es bueno	it is good
es fácil	it is likely
es malo	it is bad
es difícil	it is unlikely
es hora de	it is time to
es dudoso	it is doubtful

Examples:

Es necesario que ella llegue a clase a tiempo.
It is necessary that she arrive to class on time.

Es necesario llegar a clase a tiempo.
It is necessary to arrive to class on time.

The following expressions of certainty do not take the subjunctive unless they are preceded by *no*:

es cierto	it is certain
es verdad	it is true
es claro	it is evident (clear)
es evidente	it is evident

Examples:

Es verdad que ella <u>va</u> todas las semanas.
It is true that she goes every week.

No es verdad que ella <u>vaya</u> todas las semanas.
It is not true that she goes every week.

Exercises: Use the the indicative, the subjunctive, or the infinitive of the verbs in parentheses. Pay close attention to the tenses.

1. Era importante que ella _____ el trabajo ayer. (terminar)

2. Es probable que Ernesto _____ ir al museo esta tarde. (desear)

3. Es fácil _____ cuando hay poco tráfico. (manejar)

4. Es dudoso que nosotras _____ pagar la matrícula de la universidad. (poder)

5. No es cierto que _____ tanto que hacer. (haber)

6. Era importante que yo _____ a visitar a mis padres. (ir)

7. Es preciso que ustedes _____ lo necesario. (hacer)

8. Es evidente que él _____ ir con nosotros. (querer)

9. Es imposible que yo _____ este trabajo esta noche. (terminar)

10. Es una lástima que ella _____ tan pedante. (ser)

6.3 The subjunctive in adjective clauses

Dependent clauses are classified as adjective clauses when they modify an antecedent.

6.3.1 The subjunctive used with indefinites

The subjunctive must be used in adjective clauses after a relative pronoun when reference is made to persons, things, or ideas that are unknown, indefinite, uncertain, or nonexistent. The indicative is used when certainty exists.

Examples:

Busco un secretario que <u>sepa</u> español.
I am looking for a secretary who knows Spanish.

Tengo un secretario que <u>sabe</u> español.
I have a secretary who knows Spanish.

Exercises: Complete the following sentences with the correct form of the indicative or the subjunctive of the verbs in parentheses. Pay close attention to the verb tenses.

1. ¿Conoces a la chica que _____ aquí? (vivir)

2. ¿Tiene algún libro que _____ interesante? (ser)

3. No hay nadie que _____ tan ocupado como tú. (estar)

4. Busco un apartamento que _____ dos baños. (tener)

5. Necesito un abogado que _____ japonés. (hablar)

6. Busco a los dos hombres que _____ bien. (trabajar)

7. Queremos encontrar un periódico que _____ el concierto del sábado. (anunciar)

8. Nos gustaría que Elena _____ con un chico simpático. (salir)

9. Hay una chica en la clase que siempre _____ las respuestas. (saber)

10. No conozco a nadie que _____ ir contigo al baile. (querer)

6.3.2 The subjunctive after indefinites

The indefinites *cualquiera*, *quienquiera*, *comoquiera*, *cuandoquiera*, and *dondequiera* are followed by *que* and the subjunctive if indefiniteness is implied. When indefiniteness does not exist, these indefinite words are followed by the indicative.

Examples:

Te buscaré dondequiera que vayas.
I will look for you wherever you may go.

La madre seguía al hijo dondequiera que él iba.
The mother followed the son wherever he went.

Exercises: Translate the following sentences:

1. Whichever car you choose will make you happy.

   _____

2. I will not speak with whomever comes.

   _____

3. He will not accept whomever you send.

   _____

4. The groom followed the bride wherever she went.

   _____

5. However he answers, don't say anything.

   _____

6.4 The subjunctive in adverbial clauses

The dependent clause is classified as an adverbial clause when the clause performs the function of an adverb. The indicative or the subjunctive may be used in adverbial clauses. The use of the subjunctive or of the indicative is determined by whether the content of the clause is a fact (indicative) or not (subjunctive).

6.4.1 Conjunctions of time that take the indicative or the subjunctive

The indicative is used after certain conjunctions if the event referred to has taken place or is certain to take place. The subjunctive is used to refer to events that have not taken place, are pending, or are regarded as uncertain. The following conjunctions may take either the indicative or the subjunctive:

después de que	after
hasta que	until
mientras que	while
luego que	as soon as
cuando	when
en cuanto	as soon as
tan pronto como	as soon as
como	as
según	according to
donde	where

Examples:

Me avisaron tan pronto como llegaron.
They told me as soon as they arrived.

Avísame tan pronto como lleguen.
Let me know as soon as they arrive.

Exercises: Use the correct form of the indicative or the subjunctive of the verbs in parentheses. Pay close attention to the tenses.

1. Toma esta medicina hasta que te _____ mejor. (sentir)

2. Siempre tomas la medicina hasta que te _____ mejor. (sentir)

3. Él apagó el televisor tan pronto como él _____. (venir)

4. Apagará el televisor tan pronto como él _____ . (venir)

5. Siempre compra donde _____ los mejores precios. (ofrecer)

6. Comprará donde _____ los mejores precios. (ofrecer)

7. Cuando Ricardo _____ te llamaré. (llegar)

8. Cuando Ricardo _____ ayer te llamé. (llegar)

9. Estudiará hasta que _____ todas las fechas históricas. (aprender)

10. Estudió hasta que _____ todas las fechas históricas. (aprender)

11. Voy aunque mañana _____ muchísimo. (llover)

12. Voy aunque ahora _____ muchísimo. (llover)

13. Lo hago siempre según ellos me _____. (decir)

14. No sé qué me dirán, pero lo voy a hacer según ellos me _____. (decir)

6.4.2 Adverbial clauses that take either the subjunctive or the indicative

The subjunctive is always used after conjunctions that express a purpose or intent, restriction, negative result, supposition, proviso, exception, concession, denial, or unfulfilled time. The following are examples of conjunctions that introduce events or actions that have not taken place and are always followed by the subjunctive:

a menos que	unless
a fin (de) que	in order that
antes (de) que	before
para que	in order that
sin que	without
en caso de que	in case that
con tal que	provided that

The infinitive is used after *para, sin*, and *antes de*.

The following conjunctions always take the indicative:

como	since
ahora que	now that
porque	because
desde que	since (time)
pues	since
ya que	now that
puesto que	inasmuch as, since

Examples:

A menos que ellos llamen, yo no iré.
Unless they call, I will not go.

Como ella no se siente bien, no puede ir.
Since she does not feel well, she cannot go.

Exercises: Use the infinitive, the indicative, or the subjunctive of the verbs in parentheses. Pay close attention to the tenses.

1. Llámame antes de que Alberto _____. (salir)

2. No podemos ganar el partido de baloncesto sin _____. (jugar)

3. Le daré el dinero a ella con tal que lo _____. (necesitar)

4. Puesto que _____ tanto, no lo podemos comprar. (valer)

5. Ya que tú _____ , ¿puedes traerme lo que necesito? (ir)

6. Perdimos el tren, porque _____ tarde. (llegar)

7. Se lo dijo a fin de que _____ la verdad. (saber)

8. ¿Puede hacerlo sin que sus padres lo _____? (saber)

9. Ahora que nosotros lo _____ mejor, lo apreciamos más. (conocer)

10. Antes de que _____ la dirección, te la quiero dar. (olvidar)

11. Llamo para _____ una reservación. (hacer)

12. Lo hizo sin _____ nada. (decir)

6.5 The subjunctive in independent clauses

The subjunctive in independent clauses occurs whenever the subjunctive is used without a preceding governing word. Expressions of this character may be considered elliptical since a governing word may be supplied to relate a wish or command or to refer to a possibility.

6.5.1 The subjunctive used with *ojalá*, *quizás*, *acaso*, and *tal vez*

The interjection *ojalá* is always followed by the subjunctive. If the verb is in the present, its English equivalent is *I hope*; if in the past, *I wish*. *Ojalá* is also translated into English as *Let's hope that.* . . . The adverbs *quizás*, *acaso*, and *tal vez* have the English equivalent of *perhaps* and use the subjunctive when the speaker feels considerable doubt. Otherwise, the indicative is used.

Examples:

Ojalá regresen temprano.
I hope they return early.

Ojalá pudiéramos ir.
I wish we could go.

¡Ojalá que tengamos un buen fin de semana!
Let's hope that we have a good weekend!

Quizás ellas reciban la invitación, pero lo dudo.
Perhaps they will receive the invitation, but I doubt it.

Tal vez él venga mañana.
Perhaps he will come tomorrow.

Exercises: Write the correct form of the indicative or the subjunctive of the verbs in parentheses.

1. Tal vez él _____ esta noche. No sé. (salir)

2. Ojalá que ustedes _____ las bebidas. (traer [I wish])

3. ¿Acaso ellos ya _____ la información? Creo que sí. (saber)

4. ¿Hará calor mañana? No sé, tal vez _____ y _____ la temperatura. (llover, refrescar)

5. Ojalá que Ricardo _____ antes de salir. (llamar [I hope])

6. Te la _____ mañana, tal vez. (dar)

7. Ojalá que tú _____ buenas notas en los exámenes finales. (sacar [I hope])

8. Tal vez yo _____ a alguien en la recepción. (conocer)

9. ¿Quizás tú _____ que hacer las reservaciones antes de partir? Sí. (tener)

10. Tal vez tú _____ la verdad, pero yo lo dudo. (decir)

6.5.2 The imperfect subjunctive and polite requests

The imperfect subjunctive is used to make polite requests.

Examples:

Quiero ir.
I want to go.

Quisiera ir.
I would like to go.

Exercises: Translate the following sentences into Spanish.

1. I would like to buy you a gift.

2. I want to visit the students.

   _____

3. I would like to send these letters to my cousins.

   _____

6.5.3 The subjunctive used as an imperative

The subjunctive is used as an imperative in the following cases when no governing word is expressed:

a) when a wish or command is conveyed as a message through one person to another.

Example:

> *Que no entre nadie.*
> Let no one in.

b) when the wish or command is not conveyed as a message but expressed indefinitely about some person or thing not present.

Example:

> *¡Que se hunda el mundo!*
> Let the world sink!

c) when the command is addressed to a person who is present.

Example:

> *Hable más alto.*
> Speak louder.

d) to convey a general permission.

Example:

> *Que digan lo que quieran.*
> Let them say what they want.

e) to indicate doubt.

Example:

> *¡Que trabaje aquí un médico tan bueno!*
> To think that such a good doctor works here!

Exercises: Translate the following sentences.

1. Let the children swim!

   _____

2. To think that such an important person lives here!

   _____

3. Let no one eat the pie.

   _____

4. Buy the house, cost what it may.

   _____

5. Say something.

   _____

6.6 The past subjunctive in *if*-clauses and after *como si*

The imperfect subjunctive is always used in *if*-clauses when a contrary-to-fact statement is made. The main clause that states the improbable or contrary-to-fact outcome takes the conditional. When an *if*-clause is not contrary to fact, the indicative is used in the *if*-clause and in the main clause. The present subjunctive is never used with an *if*-clause.

Examples:

> *Si tengo dinero, te compraré un coche.*
> If I have money, I will buy you a car.

> *Si tuviera dinero, te compraría un coche.*
> If I had money, I would buy you a car.

> *Si hubiera tenido dinero, te habría comprado un coche.*
> If I had had money, I would have bought you a car.

The imperfect subjunctive is used after *como si* since *this conjunction refers to something contrary to fact.*

Example:

Se comporta como si fuera el gerente.
He behaves as if he were the manager.

Exercises: Write the correct form of the subjunctive, the indicative, or the conditional of the verbs in parentheses.

1. Si termino de leer este libro, te _____. (llamar)

2. Si _____, ¿podrías traer los discos que te pedí? (venir)

3. ¿Se lo habrías dado si lo _____ tenido? (haber)

4. Ustedes gastan dinero como si _____ millonarios. (ser)

5. Nosotros _____ a nuestros abuelos si _____ enfermos. (visitar, estar)

6. Si ellos lo _____, te lo dirían. (saber)

7. Si tú _____ temprano de la oficina, te visitaré. (salir)

8. Si Alfredo _____ una novia, saldría todos los días. (tener)

9. Si el director me _____ una semana de vacaciones, iría a Marruecos. (dar)

10. Te _____, si Gustavo me devolviera el dinero. (pagar)

11. Si hubieran ido a clase, ellos _____ sabido la nota. (haber)

12. Si yo _____ antes que tú, te llamo. (llegar)

13. Si nosotros _____ hacerlo, lo haríamos. (poder)

14. Si hubieras pagado la cuenta, ellos no te _____ cortado el servicio telefónico. (haber)

15. Te invito a la cena, si _____ llegar temprano. (prometer)

✓ **Check Yourself**

6.2.1 **(The subjunctive after verbs of emotion, feeling, and hope)**

1. vengas 2. regalaran 3. esté 4. cante 5. saber 6. haya 7. pasara 8. sea 9. recibiera 10. tengan
11. puedas 12. rompiera

6.2.2 **(The subjunctive after verbs of volition)**

1. vayan 2. ahorrara 3. visite 4. tengan 5. ver 6. escribir 7. estudiara 8. supiera 9. obtengan 10. dar
11. bañe

6.2.3 **(The subjunctive after verbs of uncertainty, doubt, or denial)**

1. tengan 2. podían/pudieron 3. dijeron/decían 4. conoce 5. dejaron 6. irán 7. son 8. estudian
9. habla 10. mejoren

6.2.4 **(The subjunctive with impersonal expressions)**

1. terminara 2. desee 3. manejar 4. podamos 5. haya 6. fuera 7. hagan 8. quiere 9. termine 10. sea

6.3.1 **(The subjunctive used with indefinites)**

1. vive 2. sea 3. esté 4. tenga 5. hable 6. trabajan 7. anuncie 8. saliera 9. sabe 10. quiera

6.3.2 **(The subjunctive after indefinites)**

1. Cualquier carro que escojas te hará feliz. 2. No hablaré con quienquiera que venga. 3. No aceptará a
cualquiera que le mandes. 4. El novio siguió a la novia dondequiera que ella fue. 5. Comoquiera que
conteste, no digas/diga nada.

6.4.1 **(Conjunctions of time that take the indicative or the subjunctive)**

1. sientas 2. sientes 3. vino 4. venga 5. ofrecen 6. ofrezcan 7. llegue 8. llegó 9. aprenda
10. aprendió 11. llueva 12. llueve 13. dicen 14. digan

6.4.2 **(Adverbial clauses that take either the subjunctive or the indicative)**

1. salga 2. jugar 3. necesite 4. vale 5. vas 6. llegamos 7. supiera 8. sepan 9. conocemos 10. olvide
11. hacer 12. decir

6.5.1 **(The subjunctive used with *ojalá*, *quizás*, *acaso*, and *tal vez*)**

1. salga 2. trajeran 3. saben 4. llueva, refresque 5. llame 6. doy/daré/voy a dar 7. saques 8. conozca
9. tienes 10. digas

6.5.2 **(The imperfect subjunctive and polite requests)**

1. Quisiera comprarte un regalo. 2. Quiero visitar a los estudiantes. 3. Quisiera enviarles estas cartas a
mis primos.

6.5.3 **(The subjunctive used as an imperative)**

1. ¡Que naden los niños! 2. ¡Que una persona tan importante viva aquí! 3. Que nadie coma el pastel.
4. Compren la casa, cueste lo que cueste. 5. Diga algo.

6.6 **(The past subjunctive in *if*-clauses and after *como si*)**

1. llamaré/llamo 2. vinieras 3. hubieras 4. fueran 5. visitaríamos, estuvieran 6. supieran 7. sales
8. tuviera 9. diera 10. pagaría 11. habrían 12. llego 13. pudiéramos 14. habrían 15. prometes

Grade Yourself

Circle the numbers of the questions you missed, then fill in the total incorrect for each topic. If you answered more than three questions incorrectly, you need to focus on that topic. (If a topic has less than three questions and you had at least one wrong, we suggest you study that topic also. Read your textbook, a review book, or ask your teacher for help.)

Subject: Uses of the Subjunctive

Topic	Question Numbers	Number Incorrect
The subjunctive after verbs of emotion, feeling, and hope	**6.2.1:** 1, 2, 3, 4, 5, 6, 7, 8, 9, 10, 11, 12	
The subjunctive after verbs of volition	**6.2.2:** 1, 2, 3, 4, 5, 6, 7, 8, 9, 10, 11	
The subjunctive after verbs of uncertainty, doubt, or denial	**6.2.3:** 1, 2, 3, 4, 5, 6, 7, 8, 9, 10	
The subjunctive with impersonal expressions	**6.2.4:** 1, 2, 3, 4, 5, 6, 7, 8, 9, 10	
The subjunctive used with indefinites	**6.3.1:** 1, 2, 3, 4, 5, 6, 7, 8, 9, 10	
The subjunctive after indefinites	**6.3.2:** 1, 2, 3, 4, 5	
Conjunctions of time that take the indicative or the subjunctive	**6.4.1:** 1, 2, 3, 4, 5, 6, 7, 8, 9, 10, 11, 12, 13, 14	
Adverbial clauses that take either the subjunctive or the indicative	**6.4.2:** 1, 2, 3, 4, 5, 6, 7, 8, 9, 10, 11, 12	
The subjunctive used with *ojalá*, *quizás*, *acaso*, and *tal vez*	**6.5.1:** 1, 2, 3, 4, 5, 6, 7, 8, 9, 10	
The imperfect subjunctive and polite requests	**6.5.2:** 1, 2, 3	
The subjunctive used as an imperative	**6.5.3:** 1, 2, 3, 4, 5	
The past subjunctive in *if*-clauses and after *como si*	**6.6:** 1, 2, 3, 4, 5, 6, 7, 8, 9, 10, 11, 12, 13, 14, 15	

The Commands

Brief Yourself

The command or imperative is used to give orders, make suggestions, or tell people what to do. It is used only with *tú, vosotros, Ud., Uds.*, and *nosotros. Tú* and *vosotros* have different verb forms in the affirmative and the negative.

Test Yourself

7.1 Formal commands

Formal commands are used when addressing people you normally address by using *Ud.* and *Uds.* The formal command is the same in the affirmative and the negative forms. To form this command, drop the *o* of the first person singular of the present indicative and add the following endings:

verb endings	Ud. endings	Uds. endings
-ar	-e	-en
-er	-a	-an
-ir	-a	-an

infinitive	first person present indicative	stem	Ud.	Uds.
cantar	canto	cant-	cante	canten
volver	vuelvo	vuelv-	vuel	vavuelvan
sentir	siento	sient-	sienta	sientan

The command forms of the following verbs are irregular:

    ser: sea, sean

    ir: vaya, vayan

Examples:

Voten por los mejores representantes del pueblo.
Vote for the best representatives of the people.

No sea tan impaciente.
Don't be so impatient.

Exercises: Answer the following questions in complete sentences using the *Ud.* or *Uds.* command form.

1. ¿Hablo con el director del instituto?

   No, _____

2. ¿Cerramos las ventanas de la casa antes de salir?

   Sí, _____

3. ¿Traemos la documentación a la oficina?

   Sí, _____

4. ¿Doblo a la derecha o a la izquierda?

_____

5. ¿Dónde debemos de estar a las siete? ¿En casa?

_____

6. ¿Cúando vuelvo al trabajo? ¿El lunes?

_____

7. ¿Con quién hablo? ¿Con el secretario?

_____

8. ¿Traducimos el libro del inglés al japonés o al árabe?

_____

9. ¿Cómo debo de ser? ¿Entusiasta o problemática? [use *ser* and not *deber* in your answer]

_____

10. ¿Pedimos sopa o ensalada?

_____

7.2 Familiar commands

The familiar commands are used when addressing people you normally address by *tú* or *vosotros*. The personal pronoun is rarely used with the *tú* and the *vosotros* command forms. The familiar commands have different forms in the affirmative and the negative.

7.2.1 Familiar affirmative commands

The familiar affirmative command for the second person singular *tú* is the same as the third person *él* of the present indicative. All verbs, including irregular stem-changing verbs and those verbs that have other irregularities, follow this pattern. The affirmative of *vosotros* is formed by replacing the *r* of the infinitive with *d*.

infinitive	present indicative third person singular	familiar affirmative command
hablar	habla	habla
leer	lee	lee
escribir	escribe	escribe
sentir	siente	siente
dormir	duerme	duerme

irregular forms

decir:	di
salir:	sal
hacer:	haz
ser:	sé
ir:	vé
tener:	ten
poner:	pon
venir:	ven

infinitive	familiar command *vosotros/vosotras*
tomar	tomad
poner	poned
abrir	abrid

Examples:

Lee el libro que te recomendé.
Read the book that I recommended to you.

Haz el trabajo lo más pronto posible.
Do the work as soon as possible.

Devolved las joyas robadas.
Return the stolen jewels.

Exercises: Write sentences using the affirmative imperative of *tú* and *vosotros* to request the following:

	tú	vosotros
1. abrir la puerta	_____	_____
2. apagar la radio	_____	_____

	tú	vosotros
3. decir todo	_____	_____
4. poner la copa en la mesa	_____	_____
5. sacar las fotos	_____	_____
6. ir al Museo del Prado	_____	_____
7. recordar la dirección	_____	_____
8. salir temprano	_____	_____
9. almorzar conmigo	_____	_____
10. oír lo que dice	_____	_____

7.2.2 Familiar negative commands

The negative command of *tú* has the same form as the *usted* command with an added -s. This form is equivalent to the present subjunctive. The negative of *vosotros/vosotras* has the same form as that of the present subjunctive.

negative or affirmative usted command		negative command *tú*
hable	+s	no hables
coma	+s	no comas
viva	+s	no vivas
diga	+s	no digas
vuelva	+s	no vuelvas

present subjunctive	negative command *vosotros*
toméis	no toméis
comáis	no comáis
escribáis	no escribáis
conduzcáis	no conduzcáis

Examples:

No vuelvas a decir eso.
 Don't say that again.

No comáis en ese restaurante.
Do not eat in that restaurant.

Exercises: Answer the following sentences using the *tú* or *vosotros* negative command.

1. ¿Juego afuera?

_____

2. ¿Conducimos a tu casa?

_____

3. ¿Considero lo que dice?

_____

4. ¿Vuelvo tarde?

_____

5. ¿Voy a las tiendas?

_____

6. ¿Firmamos el cheque?

_____

7. ¿Te hago el favor?

_____

8. ¿Salimos con los cantantes?

_____

9. ¿Pago con las tarjetas de crédito?

_____

10. ¿Traigo todas las cosas?

_____

7.3 Imperative *Let's*

The imperative English *Let's* is expressed in Spanish by the first person plural subjunctive. The form of the imperative is the same in the affirmative and the negative, with the exception of the verb *ir*.

hablar:	hablemos
comer:	comamos
vivir:	vivamos
ir:	vamos (affirmative)
	no vayamos (negative)

Examples:

Comamos a las nueve.
Let's eat at nine.

No comamos a las nueve.
Let's not eat at nine.

¡Vamos a la biblioteca!
Let's go to the library!

¡No vayamos a la biblioteca!
Let's not go to the library!

Exercises: Translate the following sentences.

1. Let's not listen to the music.

_____

2. Let's go out.

_____

3. Let's visit our relatives.

_____

4. Let's rent this house.

_____

5. Let's take the children to the park.

_____

6. Let's not answer the questions.

_____

7. Let's elect the best candidate.

_____

8. Let's go.

_____

9. Let's ask for the car.

_____

10. Let's not change the subject.

_____

7.4 Commands with reflexive and object pronouns

In affirmative commands, the reflexive pronouns and the object pronouns are placed after the verb and are attached to it. In negative commands, the reflexive pronouns and the object pronouns are placed in front of the verb. (See Part II, 12.2.)

Examples:

¿Le doy el cuaderno?

Sí, déle el cuaderno.

Sí, déselo.

No, no le dé el cuaderno.

No, no se lo dé.

¿Me siento?

Sí, siéntese.

No, no se siente.

In the case of the reflexive first person plural, the *-s* of *-mos* is dropped before *nos* in the affirmative.

Examples:

Acostémonos.

No nos acostemos.

Exercises: Answer the following questions using the object pronouns when appropriate. Your answer should be addressed to the person indicated within the parentheses.

1. ¿Busco un hotel de lujo? (tú)

   No, _____.

2. ¿Le enviamos la carta al senador? (Uds.)

   Sí, _____.

3. ¿Me siento aquí? (Ud.)

   No, _____.

4. ¿Nos vamos? (nosotros)

   Sí, _____.

5. ¿Conducimos el coche? (vosotros)

   No, _____.

6. ¿Le compro las flores a mi esposa? (tú)

   Sí, _____.

7. ¿Cuento el chiste? (Ud.)

   Sí, _____.

8. ¿Nos quitamos los guantes? (nosotros)

   No, _____.

9. ¿Repetimos la pregunta? (Uds)

   Sí, _____.

10. ¿Peinamos a las niñas?

    No, _____.

✓ Check Yourself

7.1   **(Formal commands)**

1. no hable con el director del instituto. 2. cierren las ventanas antes de salir. 3. traigan la documentación. 4. Doble a la derecha/izquierda. 5. Estén en casa. 6. Vuelva el lunes. 7. Hable con el secretario. 8. Traduzcan el libro al japonés/árabe. 9. Sea entusiasta/problemática. 10. Pidan sopa/ensalada.

7.2.1   **(Familiar affirmative commands)**

1. Abre la puerta. / Abrid la puerta. 2. Apaga la radio. /Apagad la radio. 3. Di todo. / Decid todo. 4. Pon la copa en la mesa. / Poned la copa en la mesa. 5. Saca las fotos. / Sacad las fotos. 6. Vé al Museo del Prado. / Id al Museo del Prado. 7. Recuerda la dirección. / Recordad la dirección. 8. Sal temprano. / Salid temprano. 9. Almuerza conmigo. / Almorzad conmigo. 10. Oye lo que dice. / Oíd lo que dice.

7.2.2   **(Familiar negative commands)**

1. No juegues afuera. 2. No conduzcáis a mi casa. 3. No consideres lo que dice. 4. No vuelvas tarde. 5. No vayas a las tiendas. 6. No firméis el cheque. 7. No me hagas el favor. 8. No salgáis con los cantantes. 9. No pagues con las tarjetas de crédito. 10. No traigas todas las cosas.

7.3   **(Imperative *Let's*)**

1. No escuchemos la música. 2. Salgamos. 3. Visitemos a nuestros parientes. 4. Alquilemos esta casa. 5. Llevemos/Saquemos a los niños al parque. 6. No contestemos las preguntas. 7. Elijamos al mejor candidato. 8. ¡Vamos! 9. Pidamos el coche. 10. No cambiemos de tema.

7.4   **(Commands with reflexive and object pronouns)**

1. No, no lo busques. 2. Sí, envíensela. 3. No, no se siente ahí. 4. Sí, vámonos. 5. No, no lo conduzcáis.
6. Sí, cómpraselas. 7. Sí, cuéntelo. 8. No, no nos los quitemos. 9. Sí, repítanla. 10. No, no las peinen.

Grade Yourself

Circle the numbers of the questions you missed, then fill in the total incorrect for each topic. If you answered more than three questions incorrectly, you need to focus on that topic. (If a topic has less than three questions and you had at least one wrong, we suggest you study that topic also. Read your textbook, a review book, or ask your teacher for help.)

Subject: The Commands

Topic	Question Numbers	Number Incorrect
Formal commands	**7.1:** 1, 2, 3, 4, 5, 6, 7, 8, 9, 10	
Familiar affirmative commands	**7.2.1:** 1, 2, 3, 4, 5, 6, 7, 8, 9, 10	
Familiar negative commands	**7.2.2:** 1, 2, 3, 4, 5, 6, 7, 8, 9, 10	
Imperative *Let's*	**7.3:** 1, 2, 3, 4, 5, 6, 7, 8, 9, 10	
Commands with reflexive and object pronouns	**7.4:** 1, 2, 3, 4, 5, 6, 7, 8, 9, 10	

Infinitives and Participles

8

Brief Yourself

Infinitives and participles are the nonconjugated forms of the verbs.

Test Yourself

8.1 Infinitives

Infinitives are often used as nouns and sometimes are preceded by the article *el*. They can serve as the subject, direct object of a verb, or the object of a preposition. In English the present participle is generally used as a noun in place of the infinitive.

hablar	to talk
comer	to eat
vivir	to live

8.1.1 Infinitives as subjects

The infinitive can be used as a subject of the sentence.

Example:

Encontrar el regalo perfecto requiere mucho tiempo.
Finding the perfect gift requires a lot of time.

Exercises: Translate the words in parentheses.

1. _____ otras lenguas requiere gran esfuerzo. (Learning)

2. _____ mucho dinero es la meta de muchos. (Earning)

3. _____ es muy saludable. (Running)

4. _____ mucho produce ansiedad. (Working)

5. _____ en el extranjero tiene sus ventajas. (Studying)

6. _____ y _____ causa muchos accidentes. (Drinking, driving)

7. _____ para _____. (Seeing, believing)

8. _____ diariamente alarga la vida. (Walking)

9. El _____ aumenta nuestra preparación. (Traveling)

10. _____ es malo para la salud. (Smoking)

11. _____ bien ayuda en la universidad. (Writing)

12. _____ contigo es fastidioso. (Going shopping)

8.1.2 Infinitives as direct objects

The infinitive can be used as the direct object in a sentence.

Example:

Quiero estudiar otras lenguas.
I want to study other languages.

Exercises: Translate the words in parentheses.

1. Casi todos odian _____ que levantarse temprano. (having)

2. A él no lo dejan _____ hasta tarde. (going out)

3. Ellos esperan _____ mañana. (arriving)

4. Nosotros veremos _____ el desfile este año. (passing by)

5. Vosotros sabéis _____ música latina. (how to dance)

6. Usted vio _____ el avión. (landing)

7. Esta noche oímos _____ a los estudiantes. (screaming)

8. Prefieren _____ en el aeropuerto. (waiting)

8.1.3 Infinitives as objects of prepositions

Infinitives are frequently used after prepositions.

Example:

Algunos de nosotros estudiamos para aprender.
Some of us study to learn.

Exercises: Fill in the blanks with the translation in parentheses.

1. Estudié antes de _____. (going out)

2. Vamos al parque para _____. (to rest)

3. El inglés es difícil de _____. (to pronounce)

4. Mis padres siempre tardan en _____. (to phone)

5. El abogado se fue sin _____ nada. (saying)

6. Nosotros vamos a los bares en vez de _____ a las discotecas. (going)

7. A ella la multaron por _____ en la acera. (parking)

8. Voy a trabajar después de _____. (eating)

9. Después de _____ la luz, me duermo. (turning off)

10. Estoy cansado de _____. (to wait)

11. De _____ lo que iba a pasar, no lo habríamos hecho. (knowing)

8.1.4 Other uses of the infinitive

Infinitives are also commonly used in the following situations:

a) after *que*.

Examples:

Hay que estudiar más.
One ought to (should) study more.

Tienen que cortar la hierba.
They have to cut the grass.

b) infinitive after *al* has the meaning of *on* or *upon doing something.*

Example:

Al llegar, se pusieron a hablar.
Upon arriving, they started to talk.

c) with *hacer* and *mandar*, the infinitive means *to have something done.*

Example:

Él le mandó limpiar la mesa al camarero.
He told the waiter to clean the table.

d) after verbs such *oír, ver, permitir,* and *prohibir.*

Examples:

Oí roncar a mi vecino anoche.
I heard my neighbor snoring last night.

La vi salir con otro hombre.
I saw her go out with another man.

Les prohíben beber alcohol en las calles.
They forbid them to drink alcohol in the streets.

e) after *a* to express a command.

Example:

A estudiar.
Let's study.

Exercises: Fill in the blanks with the appropriate translation of the infinitives in parentheses.

1. ¿Qué dijo el profesor al _____? (to leave)

2. Les hago _____ mucho a los estudiantes. (to read)

3. Les prohíben_____ borrachos. (to drive)

4. Te tienes que _____ mejor. (to behave)

5. Les manda _____ las computadoras a los estudiantes. (to use)

6. Al _____ a mis amigos dejo de _____. (to see, to study)

7. Le hizo _____ la situación. (to describe)

8. Mandó _____ un palacio. (to build)

9. Recomendó _____ a todos juntos. (to enter)

10. Para _____ justicia hay que _____ dinero. (to have, to have)

11. Oí _____ a mi compañero. (to sing)

12. Vi _____ a mi profesor en el cine. (to entrar)

13. Al _____ lo que te dijo me fui rápidamente. (to hear)

14. ¡A _____! (Let's drink!)

15. El padre le prohibió _____ a su novio. (to see)

8.1.5 Perfect infinitive

The perfect infinitive is formed with the infinitive of the auxiliary verb *haber* plus the past participle of the main verb. It is used to express an action prior to the action of the main verb.

Example:

Se sentó sin haber pedido permiso.
He sat down without having asked for permission.

Exercises: Fill in the blanks with the translation of the words in parentheses.

1. Se marchó sin _____ la película. (having seen)

2. Sin _____ a otra cultura es difícil entenderla. (having been exposed)

3. Después de _____ todo, se puso a llorar. (having said)

4. Está prohibido beber hasta _____ los dieciséis años. (having turned)

5. Me arrepiento de no _____ español antes. (having learned)

6. Debería de _____ la tarea antes. (have done)

7. Después de _____ tanto, conviene descansar. (having danced)

8. El _____ mucho disminuye el etnocentrismo. (having traveled)

9. Se puso contento desspués de _____ las notas. (having gotten)

10. Se graduó tras _____ todos los requisitos. (having satisfied)

8.2 Present participle

The present participle is used as an adverb that modifies the action of the main verb. It can not be used as an adjective or as a noun. (See Part I, 3.1.) The present participle is also used with certain verbs such as *estar*, *ir*, and *seguir* to express the meaning of continuation.

Example:

Ella pasó casi toda la noche leyendo.
She spent almost the whole night reading.

Exercises: Fill in the blanks with the the present participle of the verbs in parentheses.

1. Salió _____ sin despedirse. (correr)

2. Se durmió_____ la televisión. (mirar)

3. _____ despacio, es más fácil comunicarse en español. (Speaking)

4. Mi casa está situada _____ la catedral. (passing)

5. _____ tanto, vas a engordar. (Eating)

6. _____ notas en clase, se puede pasar el examen. (Taking)

7. El frío iba _____ poco a poco. (increasing)

8. Mi hermano todavía sigue _____ trabajo. (looking for)

9. Continúa _____ hasta el próximo párrafo. (reading)

10. Los inmigrantes van _____ rápidamente al nuevo país. (getting accustomed)

11. Tú andas _____ lo que dice el profesor. (repeating)

12. Ellos continúan _____ después de las cinco. (working)

13. Los estudiantes siguen _____ las maravillas de su viaje. (telling)

14. Continúa _____ y así ahorrarás mucho dinero. (working)

15. Sigue_____ y sacarás buenas notas. (studying)

16. En las fiestas continúan _____ hasta el final. (conversing)

17. Lleva más de cinco años _____ con su novio. (going out)

18. Cuando la llamo siempre viene _____. (running)

19. Anda _____ todo lo que escucha en los bares. (saying)

20. Lleva _____ muchas horas. (sleeping)

21. Vosotros no continúais _____ después de beber. (driving)

8.2.1 The present participle used to replace dependent clauses

In some cases the present participle can be used alone to replace an entire dependent clause of the main verb.

Examples:

Mientras sacaba.../Sacando la nieve, se rompió la pierna.
While he was shoveling the snow, he broke his leg.

Mientras estábamos.../Estando en México, decidimos ir al Museo de Antropología.
Being in Mexico, we decided to go to the Museum of Anthropology.

Exercises: Fill in the blanks with the present participle of the verbs in parentheses.

1. _____ el hermano menor, tenía que llegar temprano. (Being)

2. El estudiante, _____ que saca buenas notas, no va a clase. (seeing)

3. _____ por tres años, abandonó la universidad. (Having studied)

4. Me fui al cine, _____ a mis amigos _____. (leaving, arguing)

5. _____ rápido llegarás antes. (Walking)

6. No quiero estudiar _____ ellos presentes. (being)

7. Mi compañero entró en el cuarto _____ y _____. (crying, screaming)

8. _____ en la oficina, se trabaja más. (Being)

8.3 Past participle

The past participle is used in the following manner:

a) as an adjective, in which case it must agree in number and gender with the noun or pronoun that it modifies. (See Part I, 3.5.)

Example:

Le escribí una carta a mi querida familia.
I wrote a letter to my dear family.

b) as an adjective or a noun that follows the verbs *ser* and *estar*. The past participle used with *ser* forms the passive voice, indicating that the subject is being acted upon. When used with *estar* it indicates a state or condition or shows the result of an action.

Examples:

Ser: El carro fue destruido por el incendio.
The car was destroyed by the fire.

Estar: A las ocho todas las tiendas estaban cerradas.
At eight o'clock, all the stores were closed.

c) Some verbs have two forms of the past participle, one regular and one irregular. The regular and irregular forms are used, respectively, as a compound tense and as an adjective.

infinitive	regular past participle	irregular past participle
atender	atendido	atento
bendecir	bendecido	bendito
corregir	corregido	correcto

despertar	despertado	despierto
maldecir	maldecido	maldito
elegir	elegido	electo
freír	freído	frito

Exercises: Fill in the blanks with the the past participle of the verbs in parentheses.

1. Hacía frío y durmió con las ventanas
_____. (open)

2. Es un profesor_____. (boring)

3. Algunos animales del zoológico andan
_____. (loose)

4. El presidente _____ probablemente sea
_____ una vez más. (elected, elected)

5. A las seis los trabajadores ya están
_____. (awake)

6. Los clientes son _____
desde muy temprano. (waited on)

7. No me gustan las casas _____
de rojo. (painted)

8. La poesía _____
despacio se disfruta más. (read)

9 Los productos _____ en México
son de buena calidad. (made)

10. Los carros _____ son más
baratos. (used)

11. Las _____ de los precios crean
descontentos. (increases)

12. Los _____ dieron
gracias a su benefactor. (beneficiaries)

13. _____ a las grandes nevadas, se
cancelaron las clases. (Due)

14. Cada vez hay más estudiantes _____ en
aprender español. (interested)

15. Una vez _____ la relación,
ya nunca volvieron a salir juntos. (broken)

16. No me gustan las patatas _____.
(fried)

✓ Check Yourself

8.1.1 (Infinitives as subjects)

1. Aprender 2. Ganar 3. Correr 4. Trabajar 5. Estudiar 6. Beber, conducir 7. Ver, creer 8. Caminar 9. viajar 10. Fumar 11. Escribir 12. Salir/Ir de compras

8.1.2 (Infinitives as direct objects)

1. tener 2. salir 3. llegar 4. pasar 5. bailar 6. aterrizar 7. gritar 8. esperar

8.1.3 (Infinitives as objects of prepositions)

1. salir 2. descansar 3. pronunciar 4. telefonear 5. decir 6. ir 7. estacionar/aparcar 8. comer 9. apagar 10. esperar 11. saber

8.1.4 (Other uses of the infinitive)

1. salir 2. leer 3. conducir/manejar 4. comportar 5. usar 6. ver, estudiar 7. describir 8. construir 9. entrar 10. tener, tener 11. cantar 12. entrar 13. oír 14. beber 15. ver

8.1.5 (Perfect infinitive)

1. haber visto 2. haber estado expuesto 3. haber dicho 4. haber cumplido 5. haber aprendido 6. haber hecho 7. haber bailado 8. haber viajado 9. haber recibido 10. haber satisfecho

8.2 (Present participle)

1. corriendo 2. mirando 3. Hablando 4. pasando 5. Comiendo 6. Tomando 7. aumentando 8. buscando 9. leyendo 10. acostumbrándose 11. repitiendo 12. trabajando 13. contando 14. trabajando 15. estudiando 16. conversando 17. saliendo 18. corriendo 19. diciendo 20. durmiendo 21. manejando

8.2.1 (The present participle used to replace dependent clauses)

1. Siendo 2. viendo 3. Habiendo estudiado 4. dejando, discutiendo 5. Caminando 6. estando 7. llorando, gritando 8. Estando

8.3 (Past participle)

1. abiertas 2. aburrido 3. sueltos 4. electo, elegido 5. despiertos 6. atendidos 7. pintadas 8. leída 9. hechos 10. usados 11. subidas 12. beneficiados 13. Debido 14. interesados 15. rota 16. fritas

Grade Yourself

Circle the numbers of the questions you missed, then fill in the total incorrect for each topic. If you answered more than three questions incorrectly, you need to focus on that topic. (If a topic has less than three questions and you had at least one wrong, we suggest you study that topic also. Read your textbook, a review book, or ask your teacher for help.)

Subject: Infinitives and Participles

Topic	Question Numbers	Number Incorrect
Infinitives as subjects	**8.1.1:** 1, 2, 3, 4, 5, 6, 7, 8, 9, 10, 11, 12	
Infinitives as direct objects	**8.1.2:** 1, 2, 3, 4, 5, 6, 7, 8	
Infinitives as objects of prepositions	**8.1.3:** 1, 2, 3, 4, 5, 6, 7, 8, 9, 10, 11	
Other uses of the infinitive	**8.1.4:** 1, 2, 3, 4, 5, 6, 7, 8, 9, 10, 11, 12, 13, 14, 15	
Perfect infinitive	**8.1.5:** 1, 2, 3, 4, 5, 6, 7, 8, 9, 10	
Present participle	**8.2:** 1, 2, 3, 4, 5, 6, 7, 8, 9, 10, 11, 12, 13, 14, 15, 16, 17, 18, 19, 20, 21	
The present participle used to replace dependent clauses	**8.2.1:** 1, 2, 3, 4, 5, 6, 7, 8	
Past participle	**8.3:** 1, 2, 3, 4, 5, 6, 7, 8, 9, 10, 11, 12, 13, 14, 15, 16	

Special Meaning and Usage of Certain Verbs

9

9.1 *Ser* and *estar*

The verbs *ser* and *estar* translate into English as *to be* and have specific usages that are not interchangeable.

Uses of *ser*. The verb *ser* is used in the following manner:

a) to identify a subject by nationality, national origin, profession, and physical and personality traits. Note that this list refers to permanent or inherent characteristics.

Examples:

Él es cubano.
He is Cuban.

Él es de Cuba.
He is from Cuba.

Ella es dentista.
She is a dentist.

Ellos son altos.
They are tall.

Ustedes son agradables.
You are pleasant.

b) to indicate material, composition, possession, and relationship.

Examples:

La casa es de ladrillos.
The house is (made) of bricks.

Esos libros son míos.
Those books are mine.

Ella es mi mamá.
She is my mother.

c) to express time and date.

Examples:

Son las cuatro.
It is four o'clock.

Hoy es el 19 de julio.
Today is the 19th of July.

d) to indicate where an event is taking place.

Example:

La cena será en mi casa.
The dinner will be at my house.

e) to indicate with the preposition *para* for whom or for what something is intended.

Examples:

Las flores son para ti.
The flowers are for you.

La brocha es para pintar.
The paintbrush is for painting.

Uses of *estar*. The verb *estar* is used in the following manner:

a) to indicate location.

73

Example:

Los niños están en casa de los abuelos.
The children are at the grandparents' house.

b) to indicate a temporary condition or state.

Examples:

María está enferma.
Mary is sick.

¿Cómo estás?
How are you?

c) with the past participle to indicate the result of a previous action. In this case the participle is used as an adjective and agrees in gender and number with the noun.

Examples:

Las cartas están escritas.
The letters are written.

El televisor está apagado.
The television set is turned off.

d) with the gerund to form the progressive form (See Part I, 3.2).

Example:

Ellos están gastando demasiado dinero.
They are spending too much money.

e) with idiomatic expressions.

estar de viaje	to be on a trip
estar de vacaciones	to be on vacation
estar de acuerdo	to agree
estar de buen/ mal humor	to be in a good/ bad mood
estar de prisa	to be in a hurry
estar en cama	to be sick in bed

Example:

No voy a hablar con Ricardo porque él no está de buen humor.
I am not going to speak with Ricardo because he is not in a good mood.

Exercises: Write the correct form of *ser* or *estar* in the spaces provided.

1. El piso de su casa _____ de madera.

2. Ellos _____ pediatras.

3. Esa chica de pelo castaño _____ mi hermana.

4. Hoy no quiere hablar contigo porque _____ en cama.

5. Yo _____ trabajando en una compañía multinacional.

6. El novio de mi sobrina _____ antipático.

7. Usted _____ chilena.

8. El matrimonio Sánchez nunca _____ de acuerdo.

9. Felipe siempre _____ de mal humor.

10. El profesor de María Cristina _____ de Bolivia.

11. Los periódicos que están en la mesa _____ míos.

12. Nosotros _____ gastando mucho dinero durante estas vacaciones.

13. Ellos _____ de viaje hasta mediados del mes que viene.

14. El concierto _____ en el Teatro Colón.

15. La casa de Carmen _____ a medio kilómetro.

16. Susana y Mercedes _____ enfermas.

17. Las tiendas _____ abiertas.

18. ¿Qué hora _____?

19. Carlos _____ cansado.

20. El regalo _____ para la novia de Anselmo.

21. El lápiz _____ para escribir.

9.2 Uses of *haber*

The verb *haber* is used as an auxiliary verb in all persons. Whenever it is used as a main verb the third person singular is used. The forms of the third person singular of *haber* are as follows:

present	hay	there is, there are
preterite	hubo	there was, there were
imperfect	había	there was, there were
future	habrá	there will be
conditional	habría	there would be
present perfect	ha habido	there has been
pluperfect	había habido	there had been
subjunctive	haya	there is, there are
imperfect subj.	hubiera	there was, there were

Examples:

Hay muchos libros en esta oficina.
There are many books in this office.

Espero que no haya nadie en el restaurante.
I hope there is no one in the restaurant.

Exercises: Translate into Spanish the correct form of *haber*.

1. ¿_____ luz allí? (Is there)

2. ¿Qué _____ que hacer para obtener el puesto? (is there)

3. _____ tres teléfonos en mi casa. (There are)

4. Sí, _____ cuatro sillones en la sala. (there are)

5. _____ varios vasos en la mesa. (There were)

6. _____ varios boletos en la recepción del hotel. (There will be)

7. _____ una explosión muy grande. (There has been)

8. Espero que _____ suficiente comida para los invitados. (there is)

9. _____ un accidente. (There was)

10. Sin ayuda monetaria no _____ suficiente dinero para terminar el proyecto. (there would be)

9.2.1 The impersonal expression *hay que* + infinitive

The impersonal expression *hay que* + infinitive indicates obligation or urgency. The English equivalent is *one/you must* or *it is necessary*.

Examples:

Hay que levantarse temprano.
One/you must get up early.

Hay que ir en auto para llegar a tiempo.
It is necessary to go by car to arrive on time.

Exercises: Translate the following sentences:

1. One must study a great deal.

_____

2. One must use a coat to go out. It is very cold.

_____

3. It was necessary to send a telegram.

   _____

4. It is necessary to walk a mile every day.

   _____

9.2.2 *Haber de* + infinitive

Haber de + infinitive conveys the idea of what is to happen, what is probably true, or a mild obligation or necessity.

Examples:

He de ver al médico mañana.
I must see the doctor tomorrow.

La tormenta ha de pasar en unos minutos.
The storm is to pass in a few minutes.

Está sonando el teléfono. Ha de ser Carmen.
The phone is ringing. It must be Carmen.

Exercises: Translate into Spanish the following expressions in parentheses.

1. Él _____ el coche en buenas condiciones. (must have)

2. Los problemas que tienen _____ en unos meses. (are to pass)

3. Susana recibió una carta esta mañana. _____ de su novio. (It must be)

4. Mañana _____ los documentos. (I must sign)

5. La profesora _____ la semana que viene. (is to come)

9.3 Uses of *tener*

The verb *tener* has a special meaning when used with *que*. *Tener* is also used to form certain idiomatic expressions.

9.3.1 *Tener que* + infinitive

Tener que + infinitive indicates a strong necessity. It is equivalent to the English *must* when it implies *have to*.

Example:

Carlos tiene que ir.
Carlos must/has to go.

Exercises: Translate the following sentences into Spanish:

1. They have to return the videos on time.

   _____

2. She must pay the phone bill next week.

   _____

3. They have to listen to understand the lesson.

   _____

4. I have to go.

   _____

5. She had to look up her number in the phone book.

   _____

9.3.2 Idiomatic expressions with *tener*

Some of the idiomatic expressions with *tener* are:

tener ___ años	to be ___ years old
tener calor	to be warm
tener la culpa	to be to blame
tener frío	to be cold
tener éxito	to be successful
tener en cuenta	to bear in mind
tener miedo (de)	to be afraid (of)
tener ganas (de)	to feel like

tener lugar	to take place
tener hambre	to be hungry
tener prisa	to be in a hurry
tener razón	to be right
tener sed	to be thirsty
tener vergüenza	to be ashamed

Example:

Juan ha tenido éxito.
Juan has been successful.

Exercises: Translate the following sentences into Spanish:

1. The party took place at Cristina's house.

   _____

2. Bear in mind that one must make reservations.

   _____

3. They are ashamed of what they said.

   _____

4. You are to be blamed for what happened.

   _____

5. I feel like going to the movies.

   _____

6. She is afraid to ski.

   _____

7. We are successful in our business.

   _____

8. He is sleepy.

   _____

9. Alexa is nine years old.

   _____

10. Pablo and Emilio are cold.

   _____

9.4 Uses of *deber*

The verb *deber* has the following meanings:

a) when used with a noun or object pronoun it means *owe*.

Example:

Debo diez dólares.
I owe ten dollars.

b) when used in the present it has the English equivalent of *should, ought to, is to*, and *is supposed to.*

Example:

Debo ver a Teresa mañana.
I ought to (am supposed to, am to, should, ought to, have to, must) see Teresa tomorrow.

c) when used in the imperfect tense it has the English equivalent of *was to, was supposed to, should have*, and *ought to have.*

Example:

Antonio por fin compró la medicina que debía tomar.
Antonio finally purchased the medicine that he was supposed to take.

d) when used in the conditional it expresses the idea of *should* or *ought to*, implying a softened statement.

Example:

Deberías cortarte el pelo.
You ought to cut your hair.

Exercises: Translate the following sentences into Spanish:

1. I ought to see the senator.

   _____

2. Guillermo was supposed to bring the information but he forgot.

   _____

3. You should arrive earlier to your appointments.

   _____

4. I owe you ten dollars.

   _____

5. Juan is to buy the necessary ingredients.

   _____

9.5 Uses of *hacer*

The verb *hacer* has the following usages:

a) With certain expressions, it indicates the state of the weather.

Examples:

Hace frío.
It is cold.

Hacía calor.
It was hot.

Hará sol.
It will be sunny.

¿Qué tiempo hace?
How is the weather?

b) *Hace* + time expression + *que* + verb in present has the English equivalent of *for.*

Example:

Hace un mes que estoy aquí.
I have been here for a month.

c) A verb in the present, followed by *desde hace* plus a time expression, has the English equivalent of *for.*

Example:

Estudiamos en esta universidad desde hace cuatro años.
We have been studying at this university for four years.

d) A verb in the perfect tense, followed by *desde*, has the English equivalent of *since.*

Example:

Ha nevado desde anoche.
It has snowed since last night.

e) *Hace* + time expression + *que* + verb in the past tense has the English equivalent of *ago.*

Example:

Hace un mes que vino.
He came a month ago.

f) A verb in the past tense + *hace* + time expression has the English equivalent of *ago.*

Example:

Se durmió hace una hora.
He fell asleep an hour ago.

Exercises: Translate the following sentences into Spanish.

1. It is windy.

   _____

2. They called an hour ago.

   _____

3. Elena has been here since yesterday.

   _____

4. How is the weather?

_____

5. Pedro went to sleep three hours ago.

_____

6. I have been here for a week.

_____

9.6 Verbs with special meanings

There are a few verbs in Spanish that have special meanings, in addition to their regular meaning, if used in the preterite or in the imperfect.

infinitive	preterite		imperfect	
conocer	conocí	I met	conocía	I knew
costar	costó	it cost (was purchased)	costaba	it was priced
poder	pude	I managed, I succeeded	podía	I was capable
querer	no quise	I refused	no quería	I didn't want
tener (que)	tuve que	I had to	tenía que	I was supposed to
saber	supe	I found out, learned	sabía	I knew

Exercises: Translate the following sentences into Spanish:

1. I met your boyfriend last night.

_____

2. This blouse cost me 35 Dominican pesos.

_____

3. I was supposed to go to the reception, but I went to the concert.

_____

4. Did you know her name?

_____

5. I found out last night that he had arrived.

_____

6. Susana refused to go to her house.

_____

7. We managed to finish the work on time.

_____

8. I didn't buy the dress because it cost too much.

_____

9. Did you know my sister?

_____

10. Did you have to buy a new car?

_____

9.7 Verbs that call for indirect objects when they carry a special meaning

Verbs like *gustar* (to like something or someone) take the indirect object pronouns. The subject in English becomes the indirect object in Spanish, and the direct object in English becomes the subject in Spanish. Two common forms of *gustar* are *gusta* (if the subject is singular) and *gustan* (if the subject is plural).

Examples:

Me	*gusta*	*esta película.*
indirect object	verb	subject
I	like	this movie.
subject	verb	direct object

Me gustan estas películas.
I like these movies.

The following verbs follow the same pattern:

doler	to hurt
faltar	to lack, to be missing
quedar	to have something left
interesar	to interest
encantar	to delight, to love a thing
ganar	to beat
pasar	to happen
parecer	to seem

Examples:

A ella le parece importante la noticia.
The news seems important to her.

No le falta nada a Margarita.
Margarita is not missing anything.

Les ganaron.
They beat them.

Exercises: Translate the following sentences into Spanish:

1. It seems to them that they will be able to go.

    _____

2. It doesn't matter to him.

    _____

3. That doesn't interest me.

    _____

4. I need (lack) fifty pesetas.

    _____

5. I lost the game. They beat me.

    _____

6. Her arm hurts.

    _____

7. We have five dresses left.

    _____

8. I love (am delighted by) classical music.

    _____

9. It seems important to me.

    _____

10. He is interested in the experiment.

    _____

✓ Check Yourself

9.1   (*Ser* and *estar*)

1. es 2. son 3. es 4. está 5. estoy 6. es 7. es 8. está 9. está 10. es 11. son 12. estamos 13. están 14. es 15. está 16. están 17. están 18. es 19. está 20. es 21. es

9.2   (Uses of *haber*)

1. Hay 2. hay 3. Hay 4. hay 5. Había 6. Habrá 7. Ha habido 8. haya 9. Hubo 10. Habría

9.2.1   (The impersonal expession *hay que* + infinitive)

1. Hay que estudiar mucho. 2. Hay que usar un abrigo para salir. Hace mucho frío. 3. Había que enviar/mandar un telegrama. 4. Hay que caminar una milla todos los días.

9.2.2   (*Haber de* + infinitive)

1. Ha de tener 2. han de pasar 3. Ha de ser 4. he de firmar 5. ha de venir

9.3.1   (*Tener que* + infinitive)

1. Tienen que devolver los videos a tiempo. 2. Tiene que pagar la cuenta telefónica la semana que viene. 3. Tienen que escuchar para entender la lección. 4. Tengo que irme. 5. Tuvo que buscar su número en la guía telefónica.

9.3.2   (Idiomatic expressions with *tener*)

1. La fiesta tuvo lugar en la casa de Cristina. 2. Ten/Tenga en cuenta que hay que hacer reservaciones. 3. Tienen vergüenza de lo que dijeron. 4. Tiene/Tienes la culpa de lo que pasó. 5. Tengo ganas de ir al cine. 6. Tiene miedo de esquiar. 7. Tenemos éxito en nuestro negocio. 8. Tiene sueño. 9. Alexa tiene nueve años. 10. Pablo y Emilio tienen frío.

9.4   (Uses of *deber*)

1. Debo/Debería ver al senador. 2. Guillermo debía traer la información pero se le olvidó. 3. Debes/Debe llegar más temprano a tus/sus citas. 4. Te/Le debo diez dólares. 5. Juan debe comprar los ingredientes necesarios.

9.5   (Uses of *hacer*)

1. Hace viento. 2. Llamaron hace una hora./Hace una hora que llamaron. 3. Elena está aquí desde ayer. 4. ¿Qué tiempo hace? 5. Pedro se durmió hace tres horas. 6. Hace una semana que estoy aquí./Estoy aquí desde hace una semana.

9.6   (Verbs with special meanings)

1. Conocí a tu/su novio anoche. 2. La blusa me costó 35 pesos dominicanos. 3. Tenía que ir a la recepción, pero fui al concierto. 4. ¿Sabías/Sabía su nombre? 5. Anoche supe que él había llegado. 6. Susana no quiso ir a su casa. 7. Pudimos terminar el trabajo a tiempo. 8. No compré el vestido porque costaba demasiado. 9. ¿Conocías a mi hermana? 10. ¿Tuviste que comprar un coche nuevo?

9.7   (Verbs that call for indirect objects when they carry a special meaning)

1. Les parece que podrán ir./Les parece que van a poder ir. 2. No le importa. 3. No me interesa eso./Eso no me interesa. 4. Me faltan cincuenta pesetas. 5. Perdí el partido/juego. Me ganaron. 6. Le duele el brazo. 7. Nos quedan cinco vestidos. 8. Me encanta la música clásica. 9. Me parece importante. 10. Le interesa el experimento.

Grade Yourself

Circle the numbers of the questions you missed, then fill in the total incorrect for each topic. If you answered more than three questions incorrectly, you need to focus on that topic. (If a topic has less than three questions and you had at least one wrong, we suggest you study that topic also. Read your textbook, a review book, or ask your teacher for help.)

Subject: Special Meaning and Usage of Certain Verbs

Topic	Question Numbers	Number Incorrect
Ser and *estar*	**9.1:** 1, 2, 3, 4 , 5, 6, 7, 8, 9, 10, 11, 12, 13, 14, 15, 16, 17, 18, 19, 20, 21	
Uses of *haber*	**9.2:** 1, 2, 3, 4, 5, 6, 7, 8, 9, 10	
The impersonal expession *hay que* + infinitive	**9.2.1:** 1, 2, 3, 4	
Haber de + infinitive	**9.2.2:** 1, 2, 3, 4, 5	
Tener que + infinitive	**9.3.1:** 1, 2, 3, 4, 5	
Idiomatic expressions with *tener*	**9.3.2:** 1, 2, 3, 4, 5, 6, 7, 8, 9, 10	
Uses of *deber*	**9.4:** 1, 2, 3, 4, 5	
Uses of *hacer*	**9.5:** 1, 2, 3, 4, 5, 6	
Verbs with special meanings	**9.6:** 1, 2, 3, 4, 5, 6, 7, 8, 9, 10	
Verbs that call for indirect objects when they carry a special meaning	**9.7:** 1, 2, 3, 4, 5, 6, 7, 8, 9, 10	

Part II:
Other Grammatical Forms

Nouns and Articles

10

Brief Yourself

A noun is a person, place, thing, or idea that functions as a subject of a verb, a direct or indirect object of a verb, or the object of a preposition. Articles are words that accompany and modify nouns or noun equivalents. Nouns and articles agree in gender and number.

Test Yourself

10.1 Agreement of nouns and articles

Examples:

El estudiante habla muy bien el español.
The student speaks Spanish very well.

La camarera le da una taza de té a Mariano.
The waitress gives a cup of tea to Mariano.

10.1.1 Gender of nouns

All nouns in Spanish are either masculine or feminine, even inanimate objects. Most nouns ending in *-o* are masculine, and those ending in *-a* are feminine. Many nouns form the feminine by changing the final *-o* of the masculine to *-a*, others by adding *-a* to the masculine form.

Examples:

masculine	feminine
niño	niña
director	directora

Most nouns endings in *-l*, *-e*, or *-r* are masculine. Most ending in *-d*, *-ción*, *-sión*, *-umbre*, or *-z* are feminine.

masculine	feminine
el perro	la princesa

el plato	la canción
el amor	la ciudad
el color	la televisión
el comité	la costumbre
el estudio	la luz

Some common exceptions are:

a) masculine nouns with feminine endings:

el día, el problema, el lápiz, el arroz, el clima, el sistema, el tema, el mapa, el programa, el drama, el planeta

b) feminine nouns with masculine endings:

la radio, la mano, la foto, la moto, la flor, la sal

c) Nouns that end in *-ista* can be either masculine or feminine. The gender is indicated by the article used.

Examples:

La dentista de mi hermano es muy cara.
My brother's dentist is very expensive.

El dentista de mi papá es pésimo.
My father's dentist is very bad.

Exercises: Indicate if the italicized nouns are masculine or feminine.

1. Ha hecho mucho en frío los últimos *días*.

    _____

2. Siempre hay alguien que crea *problemas*.

    _____

3. Rosalía de Castro escribió *poemas* muy bellos.

    _____

4. No tengo ni *moto* ni coche.

    _____

5. Los viernes siempre hay *bailes*.

    _____

6. Terminó su *tesis* doctoral hace pocos años.

    _____

7. Ya no quedan *billetes* de lotería.

    _____

8. Muchos países están en *crisis*.

    _____

9. EE.UU. todavía está construyendo más *cárceles*.

    _____

10. No pongo *sal* en la comida.

    _____

11. Aprendimos a hacer *análisis* estilísticos.

    _____

12. En los conciertos siempre hay *muchedumbres*.

    _____

13. Sacamos muchas *fotos* en Santiago de Compostela.

    _____

14. Esta universidad tiene *programas* en el extranjero.

    _____

10.1.2 Number of nouns

Nouns are either singular or plural. Singular nouns ending in a vowel add an -*s* to become plural. Singular nouns ending in a consonant add -*es* to become plural.

singular	plural
el mango	los mango*s*
la pera	las pera*s*
el jamón	los jamon*es*
el avión	los avion*es*
el bambú	los bambú*es*

Note that nouns ending in an unstressed vowel with final -*s* do not change.

el martes	los martes
la crisis	las crisis

Nouns that end in -*z* change the -*z* to -*c* and add -*es* to form the plural.

la vez	las veces
el lápiz	los lápices

Exercises: Change the nouns from singular to plural and vice versa.

1. la tesis _____

2. las luces _____

3. la cruz _____

4. las aguas _____

5. el tocadiscos _____

6. el miércoles _____

7. el esquí _____

8. los sofás _____

9. la mamá _____

10. el menú _____

11. el café _____

12. el inglés _____

13. el paraguas _____

14. los lunes _____

10.2 The definite articles

There are four ways to say *the* in Spanish, depending on the gender and number of the nouns used.

	singular	*plural*
masculine	el	los
feminine	la	las

la changes to *el* when a feminine singular noun starts with a stressed *a* or *ha*.

Examples:

El agua de los ríos está fría en invierno.
The water of the rivers is cold during the winter.

El hambre es un problema en algunas regiones del mundo.
Hunger is a problem in some regions of the world.

Exercises: Indicate the gender of the following nouns by placing the appropriate definite article in the blank.

1. _____ sal

2. _____ azúcar

3. _____ incertidumbre

4. _____ decisión

5. _____ sistema

6. _____ libertad

7. _____ limas

8. _____ días

9. _____ fotos

10. _____ problemas

Exercises: Change the nouns and articles from singular to plural.

11. la flor _____

12. el tema _____

13. el agua _____

14. la amistad _____

15. la corbata _____

16. el lápiz _____

17. la guatemalteca _____

18. el zoológico _____

19. el alumno _____

20. la crisis _____

10.2.1 Contractions

In Spanish there are two mandatory contractions. When the prepositions *a* and *de* immediately precede the definite article *el*, they are written as one word. These contractions only occur with the article *el*.

    a + el = al   de + el = del

Examples:

Las tormentas del Caribe son peligrosas.
The storms of the Caribbean are dangerous.

Le dieron un regalo al amigo de mi novia.
They gave a gift to the friend of my girlfriend.

Exercises: Complete the sentences with the appropriate definite article. Make contractions when necessary.

1. Vieron a _____ amigos del supervisor en _____ baile.

2. _____ ventana de _____ cuarto de Julio se rompió.

3. No fueron a ___ parque porque estaba lloviendo.

4. Venimos de ___ mercado.

5. _____ clientes salieron de ___ banco.

6. ___ policía llevó a _____ borrachos a ___ cárcel.

7. Sacaron _____ maletas de ___ coche.

8. Debes darle _____ documentos a _____ profesor López.

9. Un deseo es ir a _____ Brasil. (to Brazil)

10. Ellos devolvieron los formularios a _____ bibliotecaria.

10.2.2 Uses of the definite articles

Definite articles are used in the following manner:

a) to define and determine the noun they accompany and to refer to a specific noun or nouns.

Examples:

Quiero probar el café que compraste en el mercado cubano.
I want to try the coffee that you bought in the Cuban market.

Ella es la chica que ganó la carrera ayer.
She is the girl who won the race yesterday.

b) to refer to generalized concepts or to refer to a whole group (i.e., all football games, all languages, all romantic poems, etc.)

Examples:

Me gustan los partidos de fútbol.
I like soccer games.

El turismo es muy importante para la economía española.
Tourism is very important for the Spanish economy.

Los idiomas son muy importantes.
Languages are very important.

Me gustan los poemas románticos.
I like romantic poems.

c) with the days of the week when talking about what will happen on a specific day or when generalizing about what will happen on that day every week.

Examples:

El martes vamos a esquiar en las montañas.
On Tuesday we are going to ski in the mountains.

Los domingos íbamos a las películas.
On Sundays we used to go to the movies.

d) when telling time or talking about the time.

Examples:

Son las diez de la noche.
It is ten p.m.

La conferencia es a la una.
The conference is at one o'clock.

e) Common nouns serving as the subject of the sentence must be acompanied by an article that determines the noun. This does not apply to proper nouns (i.e., people's names).

Examples:

La universidad cuesta mucho.
The university costs a lot.

La escuela abre a las ocho.
School opens at eight o'clock.

f) when referring to people with titles like *señor, señorita, señora, profesor, director, presidente, general,* etc. However, it is not used when talking directly to that person.

Examples:

El señor Arias es alto y flaco.
Mr. Arias is tall and skinny.

Voy a hablar con la directora.
I'm going to talk to the director.

but:

¿Cómo está usted, señorita Bravo?
How are you, Miss Bravo?

g) to acccompany the object of the preposition.

Examples:

Salimos de la clase muy temprano.
We leave the class very early.

Los encontré en el museo.
I found them in the museum.

h) with the names of certain countries.

Examples:

*El Salvador, los Estados Unidos, el Brasil, la
    República Dominicana, el Perú, el Canadá, el
    Japón, la Argentina*

i) with clothing and parts of the body when it is obvious who the possessor is.

Examples:

Elena se lava las manos.
Elena washes her hands.

Roberto se quita el abrigo.
Robert takes off his coat.

j) to determine the meaning of the noun.

el cura	priest	la cura	cure
el derecho	right, law	la derecha	right, direction
el fondo	bottom, fund	la fonda	inn
el mango	handle of a utensil	la manga	sleeve
el modo	way, manner	la moda	fashion
el puerto	port	la puerta	door
el suelo	ground	la suela	sole
el bando	party, faction	la banda	band
el palo	stick	la pala	shovel
el punto	dot, period	la punta	point, tip
el resto	rest	la resta	subtraction
el capital	capital (money)	la capital	capital city
el policía	policeman	la policía	police, policewoman

Examples:

*El capital invertido en el restaurante fue de diez
    millones de pesetas.*
The capital invested in the restaurant was ten
    million pesetas.

La capital está muy contaminada.
The capital city is very polluted.

k) The definite article is omitted before a numeral used with names.

Example:

Alfonso Trece
Alfonso the Thirteenth

Exercises: Complete the following sentences with the definite article. If the article is not required, mark an *X* in the blank.

1. _____valores morales se pasan entre _____ generaciones.

2. Bartolomé de las Casas fue ____ defensor de_____ indígenas.

3. _____ jóvenes están decorando _____ habitación.

4. _____ día anterior compramos _____ regalos para _____ familia.

5. ____ agua y _____ café están calientes.

6. _____ muchachos ponen _____ lápices y ____ libretas en ____ mochila.

7. . Debemos seguir _____ instrucciones que dejó ____ directora.

8. _____ civilización maya se conoce por ____exactitud de sus calendarios.

9. Ésta fue _____ primera vez que ella probó ____ sangría.

10. Benito Juárez luchó para liberar ____ país de ____ franceses.

11. _____ cinco de mayo es ____ día de ____ independencia mexicana.

12. _____ amiga de Alicia le dio _____ mano_____ profesor.

13. _____ clases empiezan _____ cuatro de septiembre.

14. Todos _____ días a _____ diez llamo a mis amigos.

15. ____ mejor estación del año es ____ verano.

16. _____ leyes son muy estrictas.

17. _____ crisis económicas desestabilizan _____ países.

18. _____ fotos de _____ últimas vacaciones salieron muy bien.

19. _____ sol del Caribe quema mucho _____ piel.

20. _____ sistema capitalista está en crisis.

21. Me lavo _____ manos.

22. El niño abrió _____ ojos para ver mejor.

23. ___ capital de _____ República Dominicana es Santo Domingo.

24. Todos nos lavamos los dientes todos _____ días.

25. ___ esposa de _____ señor Vázquez es veterinaria.

26. ____ viernes _____ estudiantes salen a divertirse.

27. _____ amistad es necesaria.

28. _____ libertad se entiende dentro de cada cultura.

29. _____ amor es bueno para _____ ser humano.

30. _____ literatura caribeña me entusiasma.

31. Son _____ nueve de _____ noche.

32. _____ amoríos son más comunes en
_____ primavera.

33. _____ naciones de_____ Caribe exportan
_____ azúcar, _____ café y _____ frutas.

34. _____ capital de _____ Argentina es
Buenos Aires.

35. Me gusta _____ tenis.

36. _____ Imperio Español decae a partir de
Felipe _____ Segundo.

37. _____ policía piensa abandonar
_____ policía.

38. _____ cura del SIDA todavía no se ha
encontrado.

10.3 The indefinite articles

Indefinite articles are used to refer to an undetermined
noun or nouns. They usually have the meaning of *a*, *an*,
or *one* in the singular and *some* in the plural.

	singular	*plural*
masculine	un	unos
feminine	una	unas

Note that *una* changes to *un* when a feminine
singular noun starts with a stressed *a* or *ha*.

un águila	*unas* águilas
un hada	*unas* hadas

Examples:

Hay unos postres en la nevera.
There are some desserts in the refrigerator.

Uno de mis cantantes favoritos es Tito Rojas.
One of my favorite singers is Tito Rojas.

Tengo una hermana que vive en Veracruz.
I have a sister who lives in Veracruz.

Exercises: Complete the following sentences with
the appropriate indefinite article.

1. La sangría es _____ bebida
deliciosa.

2. Quiero decorar la oficina con
_____ plantas.

3. Tengo _____ amigas chilenas que
cocinan muy bien.

4. La directora necesita _____ secretario
bilingüe.

5. Rubén Blades es _____ cantante
panameño.

6. Voy a contarte _____ secretos.

7. Costa Rica es _____ país
centroamericano.

8. Hay _____ edificios, _____ tiendas y __
almacén cerca de mi casa.

9. Hay _____ mosca en _____ ventana.

10. ¿Les gustaría comer _____ pasteles
riquísimos?

10.3.1 Uses of the indefinite articles

The indefinite article is not as commonly used in Spanish as it is in English. Unlike English, the indefinite
article is omitted with the verb *ser* and before an un-
modified noun expressing nationality, profession, rank,
or religion. However, when used with adjectives, the
indefinite article follows *ser* or precedes the adjective.

Examples:
Ella es actriz.   but: *Ella es una actriz famosa.*
She is an actress.   She is a famous actress.

Él es guatemalteco. but: *Él es <u>un</u> guatemalteco interesante.*

He is Guatemalan. He is an interesting Guatemalan.

In the singular, the indefinite article conveys the meaning of *one,* while in the plural it means *some.* When the indefinite article is used before the noun, it can also mean *approximately.*

Examples:

Ella no tiene una hermana sino tres.
She doesn't have one sister but three.

Hay unos inquilinos muy ruidosos en el edificio.
There are some very noisy tenants in the building.

Ellos esperan ganar unos doscientos dólares.
They hope to earn about two hundred dollars.

Exercises: Complete the sentences with the appropriate indefinite article. If the article is not required, mark an *X* in the blank.

1. La ciudad de Querétaro tiene _____ edificios coloniales preciosos.

2. Tengo _____ hambre canina.

3. No tengo ni _____ peso.

4. Juan Luis Guerra es _____ dominicano muy famoso.

5. Él es _____ persona muy responsable.

6. Hace _____ meses que no duermo bien.

7. Tengo _____ regalos para mi familia.

8. _____ día de éstos, te voy a enseñar a conducir.

9. Hay _____ blusas y faldas bien bonitas en la tienda.

10. En la sala de clase hay _____ quince estudiantes.

11. Mi hermano es _____ negociante pésimo.

12. Busco _____ casa que tenga buena calefacción.

13. _____ políticos son más corruptos que otros.

14. Tengo _____ amiga en Guanajuato, _____ de las ciudades más bonitas de México.

15. Acabó sus estudios y ahora es _____ maestra.

10.4 The neuter article *lo*

Lo is a neuter article that is used with the masculine singular form of adjectives to express an abstract idea or quality. In English the equivalent of *lo* is represented by the article *the* and the words *thing* or *part.*

Examples:

Lo bueno de este restaurante es el café.
The good thing about this restaurant is the coffee.

Lo mejor de mi pueblo son las actividades culturales.
The best thing about my town are the cultural activities.

Exercises: Provide the Spanish equivalents for the words in parentheses.

1. _____ fue cuando él empezó a contar chistes. (The funny thing)

2. _____ de la comida gallega es el aceite. (The bad thing)

3. _____ de todo fue no pasar el examen. (The worst thing)

4. _____ de estudiar lenguas es la gramática. (The boring part)

5. _____ es poder pagar la matrícula. (The difficult part)

6. _____ de Cuba es que no va a tener una solución fácil. (The sad thing)

7. _____ del viaje fue conocer a la gente. (The interesting part)

8. Hace calor, _____es que está lloviendo. (the uncomfortable part)

9. En esos casos, _____ es estar tranquilo. (the best thing)

10. La comida es _____ de las fiestas. (the good part)

11. Nosotros creemos_____ que ustedes. (the same thing)

10.4.1 *Lo* + adjective or adverb + *que*

Lo + adjective or adverb + *que* translates into English with the expression *how*. It is also used with past participles or a possessive to express abstract nouns.

Example:

Lo confuso es cuando todos hablan al mismo tiempo. The confusing part is when they all talk at the same time.

Exercises: Provide the Spanish equivalents for the words in parentheses.

1. Me sorprende_____ que es esta clase. (how boring)

2. Me habían avisado ya de _____ que era esa persona. (how fun)

3. No puedo creer _____ que se levantan los estadounidenses. (how early)

4. Deben entender _____ que yo estoy. (how tired)

5. No me gusta _____ que tú eres. (how daring)

6. Me molesta _____ que es tu personalidad. (how strong)

7. _____ a mano tiene más mérito artístico. (What is done)

8. _____ ya no tiene solución. (What happened)

9. _____ es _____. (What is mine, what is yours)

Check Yourself

10.1.1 (Gender of nouns)

1. masculine 2. masculine 3. masculine 4. feminine 5. masculine 6. feminine 7. masculine
8. feminine 9. feminine 10. feminine 11. masculine 12. feminine 13. feminine 14. masculine

10.1.2 (Number of nouns)

1. las tesis 2. la luz 3. las cruces 4. el agua 5. los tocadiscos 6. los miércoles 7. los esquís 8. el sofá
9. las mamás 10. los menús 11. los cafés 12. los ingleses 13. los paraguas 14. el lunes

10.2 (The definite articles)

1. la sal 2. el azúcar 3. la incertidumbre 4. la decisión 5. el sistema 6. la libertad 7. los climas 8. los
días 9. las fotos 10. los problemas 11. las flores 12. los temas 13. las aguas 14. las amistades 15. las
corbatas 16. los lápices 17. las guatemaltecas 18. los zoológicos 19. los alumnos 20. las crisis

10.2.1 (Contractions)

1. los amigos, el baile 2. La ventana, del cuarto 3. al parque 4. del mercado 5. Los clientes, del banco
6. La policía, los borrachos, la cárcel 7. las maletas, del coche 8. los documentos, al profesor López
9. al Brasil 10. la bibliotecaria

10.2.2 (Uses of the definite articles)

1. los valores, las generaciones 2. el defensor, los indígenas 3. los jóvenes, la habitación 4. El día,
los regalos, la familia 5. El agua, el café 6. Los muchachos, los lápices, las libretas, la mochila 7. las
instrucciones, la directora 8. La civilización, la exactitud 9. la primera, la sangría 10. el país, los
franceses 11. El cinco, el día, la independencia 12. La amiga, la mano, al profesor 13. Las clases, el
cuatro 14. los días, las diez 15. La mejor, el verano 16. Las leyes 17. Las crisis, los países 18. Las
fotos, las últimas 19. El sol, la piel 20. El sistema 21. las manos 22. los ojos 23. La capital de la
República Dominicana 24. los días 25. La esposa del señor Vázquez 26. Los viernes, los estudiantes
27. La amistad 28. La libertad 29. El amor, el ser 30. La literatura 31. las nueve, la noche 32. Los
amoríos, la primavera 33. Las naciones del Caribe, X, X, X 34. La capital de la Argentina 35. el tenis
36. El Imperio, X 37. El/la policía, la policía 38. La cura

10.3 (The indefinite articles)

1. una bebida 2. unas plantas 3. unas amigas 4. un secretario 5. un cantante 6. unos secretos
7. un país 8. unos edificios, unas tiendas, un almacén 9. una mosca, una ventana 10. unos pasteles

10.3.1 (Uses of the indefinite articles)

1. unos edificios 2. un hambre 3. un peso 4. un dominicano 5. una persona 6. unos meses 7. unos
regalos 8. Un día 9. unas blusas 10. unos quince 11. un negociante 12. una casa 13. Unos políticos
14. una amiga, una de las ciudades 15. x

10.4 (The neuter article *lo*)

1. Lo gracioso 2. Lo malo 3. Lo peor 4. Lo aburrido 5. Lo difícil 6. Lo triste 7. Lo interesante
8. lo incómodo 9. lo mejor 10. lo bueno 11. lo mismo

10.4.1 (*Lo* + adjective or adverb + *que*)

1. lo aburrida 2. lo divertida 3. lo temprano 4. lo cansado 5. lo atrevido 6. lo fuerte 7. Lo hecho
8. Lo ocurrido 9. Lo mío, lo tuyo

Grade Yourself

Circle the numbers of the questions you missed, then fill in the total incorrect for each topic. If you answered more than three questions incorrectly, you need to focus on that topic. (If a topic has less than three questions and you had at least one wrong, we suggest you study that topic also. Read your textbook, a review book, or ask your teacher for help.)

Subject: Nouns and Articles

Topic	Question Numbers	Number Incorrect
Gender of nouns	**10.1.1:** 1, 2, 3, 4, 5, 6, 7, 8, 9, 10, 11, 12, 13, 14	
Number of nouns	**10.1.2:** 1, 2, 3, 4, 5, 6, 7, 8, 9, 10, 11, 12, 13, 14	
The definite articles	**10.2:** 1, 2, 3, 4, 5, 6, 7, 8, 9, 10, 11, 12, 13, 14, 15, 16, 17, 18, 19, 20	
Contractions	**10.2.1:** 1, 2, 3, 4, 5, 6, 7, 8, 9, 10	
Uses of the definite articles	**10.2.2:** 1, 2, 3, 4, 5, 6, 7, 8, 9, 10, 11, 12, 13, 14, 15, 16, 17, 18, 19, 20, 21, 22, 23, 24, 25, 26, 27, 28, 29, 30, 31, 32, 33, 34, 35, 36, 37, 38	
The indefinite articles	**10.3:** 1, 2, 3, 4, 5, 6, 7, 8, 9, 10	
Uses of the indefinite articles	**10.3.1:** 1, 2, 3, 4, 5, 6, 7, 8, 9, 10, 11, 12, 13, 14, 15	
The neuter article *lo*	**10.4:** 1, 2, 3, 4, 5, 6, 7, 8, 9, 10, 11	
Lo + adjective or adverb + *que*	**10.4.1:** 1, 2, 3, 4, 5, 6, 7, 8, 9	

Adjectives and Adverbs

11

Brief Yourself

An adjective modifies a noun. It says something about the quality of the thing named, indicates its quantity, or distinguishes the thing named from others. An adverb modifies a verb, an adjective, or another adverb.

Test Yourself

11.1 Agreement of adjectives

All adjectives agree in gender and number with the noun they modify. Some rules to follow:

a) Adjectives ending in *-o* in the masculine have an *-a* ending in the feminine.

masculine		feminine	
alto	tall	alta	tall
bonito	pretty	bonita	pretty

b) Adjectives ending in *-or, -án, -ón* in the masculine end in *-ora*, *-ana*, *-ona* in the feminine. Exceptions to this rule are *mayor*, *menor*, *mejor*, and *superior*. These adjectives remain unchanged in the feminine.

trabajador	trabajadora (worker)
holgazán	holgazana (lazy)
glotón	glotona (glutton)

c) Adjectives of nationality that end in a consonant in the masculine form add an *-a* in the feminine.

español	española	(Spanish)
japonés	japonesa	(Japanese)

d) Adjectives that do not fall within one of the preceding categories have the same form in the masculine and feminine forms.

débil	weak
eficaz	efficient
inteligente	intelligent

e) Number agreement of adjectives is formed in the same manner as for nouns (see Part II, 10.1).

Examples:

la chica triste
the sad girl

las chicas tristes
the sad girls

f) When an adjective modifies two or more nouns of different genders, the plural masculine form is used.

Example:

María y Juan son perezosos.
María and Juan are lazy.

Exercises: Give the correct Spanish translation of the adjectives in parentheses.

1. Carmen y María Luisa son _____.
(tall)

2. Roberto y Luis son _____ estudiantes.
(good)

3. La película que vi anoche es _____.
(French)

4. El hombre que está en la esquina es
_____. (Costa Rican)

5. Nosotros somos _____. (lazy)

6. Las hermanas de Felipe son _____.
(pleasant)

7. El boxeador que ganó la pelea es
_____. (strong)

8. Mis padres no son _____.
(conservative)

9. La secretaria y el dentista de Ricardo son
_____. (short)

10. Las hijas de María del Carmen son
_____. (intelligent)

11.1.1 Position of adjectives

Adjectives may be placed in front of or after the noun:

Adjectives follow nouns in the following situations:

a) when they are descriptive and are used to differentiate the noun from others.

Example:

el niño inteligente
the intelligent child

b) when they denote nationality.

Example:

María es una periodista chilena.
María is a Chilean journalist.

c) when they are modified by adverbs.

Example:

Leí una novela muy interesante.
I read a very interesting novel.

d) when two or more adjectives modify the same noun in a sentence.

Example:

Carolina vive en una casa grande y elegante.
Carolina lives in a big, elegant house.

Adjectives precede nouns in the following situations:

a) when they are used to enhance, give a poetic meaning, or to express a quality that naturally belongs to the noun.

Examples:

la blanca nieve
the white snow

el azul mar
the blue sea

b) when using cardinal and ordinal numbers (except with personal titles and chapters of books), possessive adjectives (short forms), and demonstrative adjectives (see Part II, 13.2).

Examples:

Tengo cinco cuadernos.
I have five notebooks.

Alberto es el primer estudiante en entrar.
Alberto is the first student to come in.

Exceptions:

Acabo de leer la lección primera.
I just finished reading lesson one.

Felipe II fue rey de España.
Philip II was king of Spain.

Exercises: Translate the following sentences into Spanish.

1. Rosa Montero is a Spanish writer.

   _____

2. I have read four novels this summer.

   _____

3. The movie we saw last night was very interesting.

   _____

4. Charles I was one of the great kings of Spain.

   _____

5. Beatriz and Rodrigo are quiet, discreet, and efficient.

   _____

6. Ramón just finished writing his fifth short story.

   _____

7. Teresa is an attractive woman.

   _____

8. He started the poem with "The blue sea..."

   _____

11.1.2 Shortened adjectives

Bueno, *malo*, *alguno*, *ninguno*, *primero*, and *tercero* become *buen*, *mal*, *algún*, *ningún*, *primer*, *gran*, and *tercer* in front of masculine singular nouns.

Examples:

el buen niño
the good child

el niño bueno
the good child

Exercises: Translate and place in the blanks the correct form of the adjectives in parentheses.

1. Ella es la _____ de su clase. (first)

2. No vino _____ estudiante. (any)

3. Mi cuñado es el _____ hombre en la fila. (third)

4. Tenemos un _____ problema. (great)

5. Vivo en la _____ casa. (third)

6. ¿Quieres algunas de estas frutas? No, gracias, no quiero _____. (any)

7. Marcos es un _____ estudiante. Nunca estudia. (bad)

8. No tenemos un _____ presidente. (good)

9. ¿Quién dijo eso? Debe de haber sido _____ hombre. (some)

10. El trabajo que hizo fue muy _____. (good)

11.1.3 Adjectives that change in meaning according to placement

Some adjectives have different meanings depending on their placement.

adjective	before noun	after noun
grande	great (gran)	large
pobre	poor (unfortunate)	poor (not wealthy)

vieja	old (of long standing)	old (elderly)
nuevo	new (different)	new (new, unused)
pura	just	pure
único	only	unique
mismo	the same	oneself/yourself/himself, etc.

Exercises: Translate the following sentences into Spanish.

1. Gloria is an old friend.

   _____

2. This water is not contaminated. It is pure.

   _____

3. Isabel is a great woman.

   _____

4. Poor Ricardo, his wife has abandoned him.

   _____

5. I just bought a brand-new car.

   _____

6. José is an old man.

   _____

7. Julieta and Cristina are unique women.

   _____

8. This is a large living room.

   _____

9. This is the new (different) book that Luis gave me.

   _____

10. We are the only ones who can do the work.

    _____

11.2 Adverbs

Adverbs may be classified as adverbs of time, place, manner, and degree.

11.2.1 Formation of adverbs

Some adverbs are independent words such as *ayer*, while others are formed by adding *-mente* to the adjective. Masculine adjectives that end in *-o* change the *-o* to *-a* before adding *-mente*. The adverbial ending *-mente* is equivalent to English *-ly*. If the adjective has a written accent mark, the adverb retains it.

Examples:

cortés	cortésmente
tranquilo	tranquilamente
callada	calladamente

Exercises: Form adverbs from the following adjectives:

1. silencioso _____

2. sincera _____

3. admirable _____

4. lento _____

5. difícil _____

6. reciente _____

7. rápida _____

8. especial _____

11.2.2 Position and usage of adverbs

Adverbs are positioned and used in the following manner:

a) Adverbs are placed before adjectives and after verbs, but variations are possible. For example, the adverb is placed immediately after the verb when the verb has an object or the adverb has a short form.

Examples:

El edificio es horriblemente feo.
The building is horribly ugly.

Ustedes hablan bien el francés.
You speak French well.

b) When two or more adverbs end in *-mente*, the suffix *-mente* is used only with the last adverb. The preceding adverbs take the feminine singular form of the adjective.

Examples:

Lo dijo cordial y elegantemente.
She said it cordially and elegantly.

Ella habla lenta y claramente.
She speaks slowly and clearly.

c) When adverbs do not modify the same word, the repetition of *-mente* may be avoided by replacing one of the adverbs with *con/de* + noun or *de una manera* and *de un modo* followed by an adjective.

Examples:

Él hizo el trabajo perfectamente y lo presentó con orgullo.
He did the work perfectly and presented it proudly.

Él escribió el informe de una manera profesional.
He wrote the report professionally.

d) Adverbs are compared by placing *más*, *menos*, or *tan* before the word compared (See Part II, 14.1).

Example:

Él comprende tan bien como yo.
He understands as well as I do.

Exercises: Translate the following sentences into Spanish.

1. Julián walked through the street rapidly and nervously.

   _____

2. Mercedes spoke cleary and presented the report professionally.

   _____

3. Pedro spoke sincerely when he said that.

   _____

4. They are eternally grateful to you.

   _____

✔ Check Yourself

11.1 (Agreement of adjectives)

1. altas 2. buenos 3. francesa 4. costarricense 5. perezosos/holgazanes/vagos 6. agradables 7. fuerte
8. conservadores 9. bajos 10. inteligentes

11.1.1 (Position of adjectives)

1. Rosa Montero es una escritora española. 2. He leído cuatro novelas este verano. 3. La película que vimos anoche fue muy interesante. 4. Carlos Primero fue uno de los grandes reyes de España.
5. Beatriz y Rodrigo son callados, discretos y eficientes. 6. Ramón acaba de terminar de escribir su quinto cuento. 7. Teresa es una mujer atractiva. 8. Él comenzó el poema con «El azul mar...».

11.1.2 (Shortened adjectives)

1. primera 2. ningún 3. tercer 4. gran 5. tercera 6. ninguna 7. mal 8. buen 9. algún 10. bueno

11.1.3 (Adjectives that change in meaning according to placement)

1. Gloria es una vieja amiga. 2. Esta agua no está contaminada. Es pura. 3. Isabel es una gran mujer.
4. Pobre Ricardo, su esposa lo ha abandonado. 5. Acabo de comprar un coche/auto nuevo. 6. José es un hombre viejo. 7. Julieta y Cristina son mujeres únicas. 8. Ésta es una sala grande. 9. Éste es el nuevo libro que Luis me dio. 10. Somos los únicos que podemos hacer el trabajo.

11.2.1 (Formation of adverbs)

1. silenciosamente 2. sinceramente 3. admirablemente 4. lentamente 5. difícilmente 6. recientemente
7. rápidamente 8. especialmente

11.2.2 (Position and usage of adverbs)

1. Julián caminó/caminaba por la calle rápida y nerviosamente. 2. Mercedes habló con claridad y presentó el informe de una manera profesional. 3. Pedro habló sinceramente cuando dijo eso.
4. Te/Le están eternamente agradecidos.

Grade Yourself

Circle the numbers of the questions you missed, then fill in the total incorrect for each topic. If you answered more than three questions incorrectly, you need to focus on that topic. (If a topic has less than three questions and you had at least one wrong, we suggest you study that topic also. Read your textbook, a review book, or ask your teacher for help.)

Subject: Adjectives and Adverbs

Topic	Question Numbers	Number Incorrect
Agreement of adjectives	**11.1:** 1, 2, 3, 4, 5, 6, 7, 8, 9, 10	
Position of adjectives	**11.1.1:** 1, 2, 3, 4, 5, 6, 7, 8	
Shortened adjectives	**11.1.2:** 1, 2, 3, 4, 5, 6, 7, 8, 9, 10	
Adjectives that change in meaning according to placement	**11.1.3:** 1, 2, 3, 4, 5, 6, 7, 8, 9, 10	
Formation of adverbs	**11.2.1:** 1, 2, 3, 4, 5, 6, 7, 8	
Position and usage of adverbs	**11.2.2:** 1, 2, 3, 4	

Pronouns

12

12.1 Subject pronouns

Subject pronouns perform the action of the verb. In English, subject pronouns are required to show who is performing the action. In Spanish, however, since conjugated verbs reflect the subject, these pronouns are used only to provide emphasis, clarity, or contrast.

yo	I
tú	you
él, ella, usted	he, she, you
nosotros, nosotras	we
vosotros, vosotras	you
ellos, ellas, ustedes	they, you

There are four ways to say *you* in Spanish. *Tú* and *usted* are singular forms that refer to one individual. *Tú* is informal and addresses friends, family, children, classmates, or anyone else in the same social category—in other words, people with whom one is on a first-name basis. *Usted* indicates formality or courtesy. It is employed when referring to strangers, older individuals, or people in important positions. *Vosotros* and *vosotras* are the plural form of *tú*. *Vosotros* is used informally in Spain, while in all other Spanish-speaking countries *ustedes* is used to address a group of people directly. *Ud.* and *Uds.* are frequent abbreviations for *usted* and *ustedes*. *Él, ella, ellos, ellas* refer only to people. There is no equivalent subject pronoun for *it* (singular or plural) in Spanish. Note that *nosotros(as)* and *vosotros(as)* have feminine and masculine forms. *Nosotras* and *vosotras* apply to all female groups, whereas *nosotros* and *vosotros* refer to mixed and all-male groups.

Exercises: Which subject pronoun would be used when *talking to* the following people?

1. your friend _____

2. your parents (in Latin America) _____

3. a classmate _____

4. the president of a bank _____

5. your sisters and brothers (in Spain) _____

Exercises: Which subject pronoun would be used when *talking about* the following people?

6. your friend's mother _____

7. your parents _____

8. your brother _____

9. your professors _____

10. yourself _____

Exercises: Complete the sentences with the appropriate subject pronoun. In cases where several subject pronouns could be used, indicate all of them.

11. _____ viene a mi casa todos los martes.

12. _____ tengo veinte años.

13. _____ comemos en la cafetería frecuentemente.

14. ¿Tocas __ algún instrumento?

15. Profesor González, ¿cómo está _____?

16. _____ quiero que me enseñen a esquiar.

17. ¿ _____ conocen a mi sobrina?

18. _____ manejamos toda la noche.

19. ¿ _____ vas a barrer el piso de la cocina?

20. ¿ _____ vais al mercado ahora?

12.2 Object pronouns

There are three types of object pronouns: direct, indirect, and prepositional.

12.2.1 Direct object pronouns

Direct object pronouns receive the direct action of the verb. They replace direct object nouns and have the same gender and number as the replaced noun.

me	me
te	you
lo, la	him, her, it
nos	us
os	you
los, las	them

Examples:

Miro la película. *La miro.*
I watch the movie. I watch it.

Hemos leído el periódico. *Lo hemos leído.*
We have read the newspaper. We have read it.

Exercises: Rewrite the following sentences using direct object pronouns.

1. Yo estudio las civilizaciones precolombinas.

   Yo _____ estudio.

2. Ella trajo los regalos.

   Ella _____ trajo.

3. Voy a llamar a mi familia por teléfono.

   Voy a llamar _____.

4. Estoy contando los ingresos del negocio.

   Estoy contándo _____.

5. Yo no creo que ellos hablen portugués.

   Yo no creo que ellos _____ hablen.

6. Haga usted la cama.

   Hága _____.

7. El autobús trae a las niñas.

   El autobús _____ trae.

8. Ella publicó un libro.

   Ella _____ publicó.

9. La secretaria mandó ordenar la oficina.

   La secretaria mandó ordenar _____.

10. Todos pedimos el menú antes de comer.

    Todos _____ pedimos antes de comer.

11. Escribimos muchas cartas este año.

    _____ escribimos este año.

12. Quería leer la novela pero no pude.

    _____ quería leer pero no pude.

13. Yo no toco la guitarra.

    Yo no _____ toco.

14. Tenemos que cortar la hierba esta primavera.

    Tenemos que cortar _____ esta primavera.

15. La directora recibió una llamada urgente.

    La directora _____ recibió.

16. ¡Escucha a tu padre!

    ¡Escúcha _____!

17. Estoy segura de que ella invitó a mi amiga.

    Estoy segura de que ella _____ invitó.

18. ¿Trajiste el artículo que te pedí?

    ¿ _____ trajiste?

19. Los niños están escuchando la orquesta.

    Los niños _____ están escuchando.

20. Teresa limpia el baño rápidamente.

    Teresa _____ limpia rápidamente.

21. ¡No cierres las ventanas!

    ¡No _____ cierres!

22. Yo preparo las maletas para el viaje.

    Yo _____ preparo.

23. ¡Lava la ropa!

    ¡Láva _____!

24. El mesero trae las bebidas.

    El mesero _____ trae.

25. Ellos ven a los chicos.

    Ellos _____ ven.

26. ¡No comas más dulces!

    ¡No _____ comas!

27. ¡Explique su idea!

    ¡Explíque _____

28. ¡No leas su carta!

    ¡No _____ leas!

12.2.2 Indirect object pronouns

Indirect object pronouns replace indirect object nouns and are used to refer to the person(s) or thing(s) receiving the direct object. They are also used to refer to the person(s) or thing(s) affected by the action of the verb. In Spanish it is common to use both the indirect object noun and the indirect object pronoun in the same sentence, especially in the third person singular and plural.

me	me
te	you
le (se)	him, her, it
nos	us
os	you
les (se)	them

Example:

Le digo las noticias al <u>profesor Martínez</u>.
I tell Professor Martínez the news.

Exercises. Complete the sentences with the appropriate indirect object pronoun.

1. ¿Estás dándo ____ los chicles a tu hermanito?

2. ¿Cuándo _____ van a preparar ceviche a nosotros?

3. ____ traen los regalos a ti.

4. ____ cuenta la historia a mí.

5. ____ doy las gracias a vosotros.

6. Estamos pagándo ____ más de lo que tú mereces.

7. El profesor Sánchez ____ exige mucho a los estudiantes.

8. ¿A ustedes ____ gustan los helados?

9. A mí ____ encantan los murales de Diego Rivera.

10. No ____ pegues a tus amigos.

12.2.3 Position of object pronouns

Object pronouns go either immediately before or directly after the verb, depending on the form of the verb used. For example:

a) With conjugated verbs (except with affirmative commands), the pronoun precedes the verb.

Examples:

<u>Le</u> gané.
I beat him.

<u>Me</u> dio dinero.
He/she gave me money.

<u>Le</u> mando un regalo.
I send him/her a gift.

b) The pronoun is placed before the auxiliary verb in perfect forms.

Examples:

<u>Le</u> he dado las herramientas.
I have given him/her the tools.

¿<u>Me</u> has dicho todo?
Have you told me everything?

c) The pronoun is placed before or after the auxiliary, the present participle, or the infinitive.

Example:

<u>Te</u> estoy explicando cómo llegar.
    Estoy explicándo<u>te</u> cómo llegar.
    I am explaining to you how to get there.

d) The pronoun is placed before the verb in negative commands and after the verb in affirmative commands.

Examples:

¡No <u>le</u> digas nada!
Don't tell him anything!

¡No <u>me</u> estropeen el cuadro!
Don't damage my painting!

Hábla<u>le</u> a ella de tus expectativas.
Tell her about your expectations.

Di<u>me</u> lo que sabes del accidente.
Tell me what you know about the accident.

Exercises: Rewrite the following sentences, substituting direct or indirect object pronouns for the objects.

1. ¡No pongan los pies en la mesa!

   _____

2. ¡No dé más excusas!

   _____

3. Paco y Susana compran los refrescos.

   _____

4. ¡Empiecen el partido!

   _____

5. He lavado los platos.

   _____

6. Estoy haciendo mis deberes.

   _____

7. ¡Háblale a Maribel!

   _____

8. ¡Ignora a Juanita!

   _____

9. El mecánico está reparando el carro.

   _____

10. Las tormentas destruyen las cosechas.

12.2.4 Double object pronouns

Direct and indirect object pronouns may be used together in a sentence in the following manner:

a) The indirect object pronoun always precedes the direct object pronoun.

Examples:

Me lo dices.
You tell it to me.

Te los devuelvo.
I return them to you.

b) The indirect and direct object pronouns may precede or follow an infinitive or a participle. When the object pronouns are attached, an accent mark must be placed on the stressed syllable of the verb in order to maintain the original stress. The accent mark is placed on the last syllable of infinitives and on the next-to-last syllable of participles.

Examples:

Quiero regalártelo.
I want to give it to you.

Está explicándonoslo.
He is explaining it to us.

c) The third person indirect object pronouns *le* and *les* change to *se* when they are combined with the third person direct object pronouns *lo*, *la*, *los*, and *las*.

		lo		se lo
le	+	la	=	se la
les		los		se los
		las		se las

Examples:

Le di el regalo al niño.   *Se lo di.*
I gave the gift to the child.   I gave it to him.

Le doy las flores a mi hermana.   *Se las doy.*
I give the flowers to my sister.   I give them to her.

Exercises: Rewrite the following sentences, substituting direct and indirect object pronouns for the direct and indirect objects.

1. ¿Me vas a sacar una fotografía ahora?

   _____

2. Le devolvió la moto.

   _____

3. El banco nos prestó el dinero para abrir el restaurante.

   _____

4. La heladaría les vende muchos helados a los turistas.

   _____

5. El mesero te está sirviendo el flan.

   _____

6. ¿Me vas a dar unas sugerencias antes de empezar?

   _____

7. Sus tíos le pagaron la cena.

   _____

8. Paz nos ha escrito una carta.

   _____

9. El cantante le va a dedicar una canción a su novia.

   _____

10. En 1999 los Estados Unidos le va a devolver el canal al gobierno panameño.

    _____

11. Le dieron el premio Nóbel a Pablo Neruda.

    _____

12. ¿Le debemos dar una llamada a Esteban?

    _____

Exercises: Answer the following questions, substituting direct and indirect objects for the direct and indirect object pronouns.

13. ¿Le vas a prestar tu tarjeta a ella?

    _____

14. ¿Ustedes nos pueden dar más tiempo?

    _____

15. ¿El jefe me va a decir la respuesta?

    _____

16. ¿Le dijeron las malas noticias al candidato?

    _____

17. ¿Os conté que tenemos que llegar a las ocho?

    _____

18. ¿Ustedes le han enseñado las instrucciones?

    _____

19. ¿Me pasas la pimienta?

_____

20. ¿Les has dicho lo que ocurrió esta mañana?

_____

21. ¿Ellos nos van a dar los recados?

_____

12.3   Prepositional object pronouns

Prepositional object pronouns are used as the object of prepositions.

mí	nosotros(as)
ti	vosotros(as)
él	ellos
ella	ellas
usted	ustedes

Note that when *mí* and *ti* are used with the preposition *con*, they become *conmigo* and *contigo,* respectively.

Examples:

Siempre piensa en mí.
She always thinks of me.

Nunca tienen una reunión sin nosotros.
They never have a meeting without us.

Nunca habló conmigo.
He never spoke with me.

¿Tus primos fueron contigo a la feria?
Did your cousins go with you to the fair?

Exercises: Complete the following sentences with the prepositional pronoun that corresponds to the subject in parentheses.

1. Los chocolates son para ____. (tú)

2. Olga no saldrá sin _____. (nosotros)

3. No quiero discutir más con ____. (tú)

4. Para ____ el viaje fue fascinante. (Jorge)

5. Las reuniones son más aburridas sin ____.
   (Alicia y Magdalena)

6. Su padre piensa mucho en ____. (José)

7. Es la bicicleta de _____. (los vecinos)

8. Para ___, el verano es la mejor estación del
   año. (yo)

9. Me alegro que hayas venido con ____. (yo)

10. Ellos salieron sin _____. (Gregorio)

12.4   Reflexive pronouns

Reflexive pronouns are used to replace nouns in sentences in which the subject and the object of a verb are the same. Reflexive pronouns follow the same placement rules as direct and indirect object pronouns. They precede single conjugated verbs, the auxiliary in perfect tenses, and only negative commands. In sentences with infinitives and present participles, they may either precede the auxiliary or they can be attached to the infinitives and present participles. Reflexive pronouns must follow and be attached to affirmative commands. The definite article is used instead of the possessive adjectives in sentences with reflexive verbs.

me	nos
te	os
se	se

Examples:

Me peino.
I comb my hair.

El chico se cepilla los dientes.
The boy brushes his teeth.

Me quito la gorra.
I take off my hat.

Exercises: Complete the following sentences with the appropriate form of the reflexive verb and pronoun.

1. Ella _____ a las siete y media. (despertarse)

2. Vosotros _____ muy elegantemente. (vestirse)

3. Mi suegro _____ demasiado. (preocuparse)

4. La mujer _____ a recoger el billete. (agacharse)

5. El muchacho _____ con cuidado para no_____. (afeitarse, cortarse)

6. Ellas _____ temprano para ir al trabajo. (levantarse)

7. No me gusta _____ con agua fría. (ducharse)

8. Mi abuelo _____ la dentadura antes de _____. (quitarse, acostarse)

9. Yo _____ mucho por mis hijos cuando llegan tarde. (preocuparse)

10. Tú _____ en hacer lo contrario de lo que te dije. (empeñarse)

12.5 Reciprocal pronouns

The reciprocal pronouns *se* and *nos* indicate reciprocal actions between two or more nouns.

Examples:

Ellos se quieren mucho.
They love each other very much.

Nos vemos a menudo.
We see each other often.

Ellos se besaron.
They kissed each other.

In case of ambiguity, *el uno al otro, la una a la otra, los unos a los otros*, and *las unas a las otras* can be added.

Example:

Las chicas se miran la una a la otra.
The girls look at each other.

Exercises: Complete the following sentences with the appropriate reciprocal pronoun.

1. Nosotros _____ escribimos cartas a menudo.

2. Uds. _____ aman muchísimo.

3. Los dos _____ cuidan mutuamente.

4. Si nosotras _____ ayudamos, podemos terminar más rápidamente.

5. Cuando mis hermanitos se enfadan, no _____ escuchan el uno al otro.

6. Los novios _____ besan tiernamente.

7. Los boxeadores _____ pegan brutalmente.

8. La abuela y los nietos _____ abrazan.

9. Edgar y yo _____ respetamos el uno al otro.

10. Los dos políticos _____ detestan el uno al otro.

✓ Check Yourself

12.1 (Subject pronouns)

1. tú 2. ustedes 3. tú 4. usted 5. vosotros 6. ella 7. ellos 8. él 9. ellos 10. yo 11. Él, Ella, Usted 12. Yo 13. Nosotros/Nosotras 14. tú 15. usted 16. Yo 17. Ellos, Ellas, Ustedes 18. Nosotros/Nosotras 19. Tú 20. Vosotros/Vosotras

12.2.1 (Direct object pronouns)

1. las 2. los 3. llamarla 4. contándolos 5. lo 6. Hágala 7. las 8. lo 9. ordenarla 10. lo 11. Las 12. La 13. la 14. cortarla 15. la 16. Escúchalo 17. la 18. Lo 19. la 20. lo 21. las 22. las 23. Lávala 24. las 25. los 26. los 27. Explíquela 28. la

12.2.2 (Indirect object pronouns)

1. dándole 2. nos 3. Te 4. Me 5. Os 6. pagándote 7. les 8. les 9. me 10. les

12.2.3 (Position of object pronouns)

1. ¡No los pogan en la mesa! 2. ¡No las dé! 3. Paco y Susana los compran. 4. ¡Empiécenlo! 5. Los he lavado. 6. Los estoy haciendo/ Estoy haciéndolos. 7. ¡Háblale! 8. ¡Ignórala! 9. El mecánico lo está reparando/El mecánico está reparándolo. 10. Las tormentas las destruyen.

12.2.4 (Double object pronouns)

1. ¿Me la vas a sacar ahora?/¿Vas a sacármela? 2. Se la devolvió. 3. El banco nos lo prestó para abrir el restaurante. 4. La heladaría se los vende a los turistas. 5. El mesero te lo está sirviendo./El mesero está sirviéndotelo. 6. ¿Me las vas a dar antes de empezar?/¿Vas a dármelas antes de empezar? 7. Sus tíos se la pagaron. 8. Paz nos la ha escrito. 9. El cantante se la va a dedicar a su novia./El cantante va a dedicársela a su novia. 10. En 1999 los Estados Unidos se lo va a devolver al gobierno panameño./En 1999 los Estados Unidos va a devolvérselo al gobierno panameño. 11. Se lo dieron a Pablo Neruda. 12. ¿Se la debemos dar?/¿Debemos dársela? 13. Sí, se la voy a prestar./Sí, voy a prestársela. 14. Sí, se lo podemos dar./Sí, podemos dárselo. 15. Sí, se la va a decir./Sí, va a decírsela. 16. Sí, se las dijeron. 17. Sí, nos lo contaste. 18. Sí, se las hemos enseñado. 19. Sí, te la paso. 20. Sí, se lo he dicho. 21. Sí, nos los van a dar./ Sí, van a dárnoslos.

12.3 (Prepositional object pronouns)

1. ti 2. nosotros 3. contigo 4. él 5. ellas 6. él 7. ellos 8. mí 9. conmigo 10. él

12.4 (Reflexive pronouns)

1. se despierta 2. os vestís 3. se preocupa 4. se agacha 5. se afeita, cortarse 6. se levantan 7. ducharme 8. se quita, acostarse 9. me preocupo 10. te empeñas

12.5 (Reciprocal pronouns)

1. nos 2. se 3. se 4. nos 5. se 6. se 7. se 8. se 9. nos 10. se

Grade Yourself

Circle the numbers of the questions you missed, then fill in the total incorrect for each topic. If you answered more than three questions incorrectly, you need to focus on that topic. (If a topic has less than three questions and you had at least one wrong, we suggest you study that topic also. Read your textbook, a review book, or ask your teacher for help.)

Subject: Pronouns

Topic	Question Numbers	Number Incorrect
Subject pronouns	**12.1:** 1, 2, 3, 4, 5, 6, 7, 8, 9, 10, 11, 12, 13, 14, 15, 16, 17, 18, 19, 20	
Direct object pronouns	**12.2.1:** 1, 2, 3, 4, 5, 6, 7, 8, 9, 10, 11, 12, 13, 14, 15, 16, 17, 18, 19, 20, 21, 22, 23, 24, 25, 26, 27, 28	
Indirect object pronouns	**12.2.2:** 1, 2, 3, 4, 5, 6, 7, 8, 9, 10	
Position of objects pronouns	**12.2.3:** 1, 2, 3, 4, 5, 6, 7, 8, 9, 10	
Double object pronouns	**12.2.4:** 1, 2, 3, 4, 5, 6, 7, 8, 9, 10, 11, 12, 13, 14, 15, 16, 17, 18, 19, 20, 21	
Prepositional object pronouns	**12.3:** 1, 2, 3, 4, 5, 6, 7, 8, 9, 10	
Reflexive pronouns	**12.4:** 1, 2, 3, 4, 5, 6, 7, 8, 9, 10	
Reciprocal pronouns	**12.5:** 1, 2, 3, 4, 5, 6, 7, 8, 9, 10	

Other Adjectives and Pronouns

Test Yourself

13.1 Possessive adjectives that precede nouns

Unstressed possessive adjectives are always placed in front of nouns and they agree in gender and number with the noun they modify.

singular	plural	
mi	mis	mine
tu	tus	your (familiar)
su*	sus	your, his, her, its
nuestro(a)	nuestros(as)	our
vuestro(a)	vuestros(as)	your (familiar)
su	sus	your, their

*Since the singular and plural forms of the third person are the same, the following forms may be used for clarification: *de él, de ella, de Ud., de Uds., de ellas, de ellos.*

Examples:

Mis amigos son de Chile.
My friends are from Chile.

Su diccionario está en casa de Pablo.
El diccionario de él está en casa de Pablo.
His dictionary is at Pablo's house.

Exercises: Translate into Spanish the possessive adjectives in parentheses.

1. Yo siempre ordeno _____ cosas. (my)

2. _____ esposa se llama Rosario. (His)

3. _____ fotos son estupendas. (Your [familiar])

4. _____ hijos estudian en la misma universidad. (Our)

5. _____ clases son por las tardes. (Your [familiar, plural])

6. ¿Quién es _____ profesora de español? (your [formal])

7. ¿Dónde están _____ cuadernos? (her)

8. Llevé a _____ amigos al cine. (my)

9. _____ casa está lejos de aquí. (Her)

10. _____ familias no se conocen. (Our)

13.1.1 Possessive adjectives that follow nouns

Possessive adjectives that follow nouns are called *stressed possessive adjectives* and have a different form than those placed in front of nouns. The stressed possessive adjectives are used to give emphasis, and agree in number and gender with the noun. Stressed possessive adjectives are usually used with the definite or the indefinite articles.

singular		plural		
masculine	feminine	masculine	feminine	
mío	mía	míos	mías	mine, of mine
tuyo	tuya	tuyos	tuyas	yours, of yours (familiar)
suyo*	suya	suyos	suyas	yours, of yours, his, of his, hers, of hers
nuestro	nuestra	nuestros	nuestras	our, of ours
vuestro	vuestra	vuestros	vuestras	your, of yours (familiar)
suyo	suya	suyos	suyas	yours, of yours, theirs, of theirs

*Since the singular and plural forms of the third person are the same, the following forms may be used for clarification: *de él, de ella, de Ud., de Uds., de ellas, de ellos.*

Example:

Yo soy una buena amiga suya/de ella.
I am a good friend of hers.

Exercises: Translate into Spanish the possessive
   adjectives in parentheses.

1. La información _____ viene de los
   periódicos. (our)

2. Esas chicas son amigas _____.
   (of mine)

3. Esos libros son _____. (yours [familiar,
   plural])

4. Este dinero es _____. (his)

5. Los amigos _____ llegaron tarde a la
   fiesta. (ours)

6. El novio _____ es abogado. (hers)

7. Los uniformes _____ son amarillos.
   (yours [familiar, plural])

8. El lápiz es ___. (mine)

9. Los cuadernos azules son _____. (ours)

10. Carolina visita a unas primas _____. (of hers)

13.1.2 Possessive pronouns

Possessive pronouns replace nouns. They agree in number and gender with the thing possessed. Definite articles usually precede these pronouns, except after the verb *ser*.

singular		plural		
masculine	feminine	masculine	feminine	
el mío	la mía	los míos	las mías	mine
el tuyo	la tuya	los tuyos	las tuyas	yours (fam.)
el suyo*	la suya	los suyos	las suyas	his, hers, yours
el nuestro	la nuestra	los nuestros	las nuestras	ours
el vuestro	la vuestra	los vuestros	las vuestras	yours
el suyo	la suya	los suyos	las suyas	theirs, yours

*Since the third person forms may be ambiguous, the following forms may be used for clarification: *el de, la de, los de, las de* followed by a third person personal pronoun.

Examples:

*Éstos son tus periódicos, los nuestros están en la
   mesa.*
These are your newspapers; ours are on the table.

¿Es tuyo? Sí, es mío.
Is it yours? Yes, it is mine.

Estas blusas son suyas/de ellas.
These blouses are theirs.

Exercises: Translate into Spanish the possessive
   pronouns in parentheses.

1. Nosotros respetamos a nuestros profesores y
   Uds. no respetan a _____. (yours)

2. Tu casa es grande y _____ es pequeña. (mine)

3. Tus padres están de viaje y _____ también. (mine)

4. Nuestras primas no están aquí de visita ni _____ tampoco. (yours [familiar])

5. Estos libros son _____ . (ours)

6. Ésta es mi chequera, _____ la dejó en casa. (his)

7. Las muñecas de Matilde y Rosario están en el patio, _____ están en la sala. (hers)

8. ¿Dónde vive la hermana de ustedes? _____ vive en Perú. (Ours)

9. Estoy contenta con mi nota, pero Roberto no está contento con _____. (his)

10. ¿Son estos sombreros _____? (yours [familiar, plural])

13.2 Demonstrative adjectives

Demonstrative adjectives agree in gender and number with the nouns they modify and are almost always placed in front of the noun.

	masculine		feminine		
	singular	plural	singular	plural	
	este	estos	esta	estas	this, these
	ese	esos	esa	esas	that, those (closer)
	aquel	aquellos	aquella	aquellas	that, those (farther away)

Example:

Este libro es mío.
This book is mine.

Exercises: Translate the demonstrative adjectives in parentheses.

1. No quiero comprar _____ pantalones. (these)

2. _____ hombre es mi tío. (That)

3. _____ personas fueron al concierto. (Those)

4. _____ chico es venezolano. (That)

5. _____ casa es de ladrillos. (This)

6. ¿Necesitas _____ cuadros para tu casa? (those)

7. No me gustan _____ sombreros de paja. (those [farther away])

8. Prefiero ir _____ mes y no el mes que viene. (this)

13.2.1 Demonstrative pronouns

Demonstrative pronouns have the same forms as the demonstrative adjectives, except that they have a written accent. The neuter form of demonstrative pronouns refers to a situation, an idea, a fact, a statement, or things that have not been named. The neuter demonstrative pronoun does not have a written accent.

masculine		feminine			
singular	plural	singular	plural	neuter	
éste	éstos	ésta	éstas	esto	this (one), these
ése	ésos	ésa	ésas	eso	that (one), those
aquél	aquéllos	aquélla	aquéllas	aquello	that (one), those (over there)

Examples:

Quiero este regalo y ése.
I want this gift and that one.

¿Qué es eso?
What is that?

Exercises: Translate into Spanish the demonstrative
pronouns in parentheses.

1. No quiero comprar estas cosas. Prefiero
   _____. (those)

2. Éste es mi dibujo y _____ es el de él.
   (that one, over there)

3. El otoño pasado fue frío pero _____ fue
   insoportable. (this one)

4. Yo no sé qué es _____. (that)

5. Esta fotografía es buena pero _____ es mejor.
   (that one, over there)

6. Susana compró estos zapatos y Carlos decidió
   comprar _____. (those)

13.3 Relative pronouns

Relative pronouns join two clauses. They refer to something previously mentioned in the sentence (the antecedent). Relative pronouns may also serve as the subject
or object of the verb, or as the object of a preposition.

13.3.1 Relative pronouns and their usages

Relative pronouns are used in the following manner:

a) The relative pronoun *que* is the most commonly used
of all the pronouns. It refers to persons and things. It is
also used after the prepositions *a*, *de*, *en*, and *con*. The
English equivalent of *que* is *that*, *which*, or *who*.

Examples:

Él llamó a la secretaria que estaba en el banco.
He called the secretary who was at the bank.

Ellos trajeron el libro que estaba en la mesa.
They brought the book that was on the table.

b) The relative pronoun *quien* (*quienes*) is used only with
persons. It is used after prepositions and in written Spanish
and replaces *que* if the relative pronoun introduces a
statement between commas. The English equivalent of
quien and *quienes* are *whom*, *that*, and *who*.

Examples:

Esa es la señora que donó el dinero.
That is the lady who donated the money.

El chico con quien bailaba era muy guapo.
The young man with whom I was dancing was very
   handsome.

c) The relative pronouns *el cual*, *la cual*, *los cuales*, and
las cuales are used in place of *que* or *quien/quienes* to
clarify one of two possible antecedents. They may be
used as a relative pronoun in nonrestrictive clauses as
subject or object of the clause and as the object of a
preposition to refer to persons and things in restrictive
and nonrestrictive clauses. Relative pronouns may refer
to persons or things. They are also used with prepositions of more than one syllable. The English equivalents
are *who* and *which*.

Examples:

La prima de Juan, para la cual compramos el regalo,
   vivió en España.
Juan's cousin, for whom we got the present, lived in
   Spain.

¿Cómo se llama el banco para el cual trabajas?
What is the name of the bank for which you work?

d) The relative pronouns *el que*, *la que*, *los que*, and *las
que* are used when a selection is implied. The English
equivalents are *the one who*, *he who*, and *those who*.

Examples:

El que ríe último, ríe mejor.
He who laughs last, laughs best.

*De todos mis libros, el que compré ayer es el más
   caro.*
Of all my books, the one that I bought yesterday is
   the most expensive.

La estudiante, la que sabía la respuesta, no la dijo.
The student, the one who knew the answer, did not
   say it.

e) The neuter relative pronouns are *lo que* and *lo cual*.
Lo que refers to a previously expressed idea and is
equivalent to the English *what*. *Lo cual* is used as subject
or object of a clause or as the object of a preposition that
refers to a previous idea. The English equivalent of *lo
cual* is *which*.

Examples:

Lo que dices es mentira.
What you are saying is a lie.

*Juan corrió en la carrera, lo cual le había prohibido
el médico.*
Juan ran in the race, which the doctor had forbidden
him to do.

f) The relative possessive *cuyo* (*cuya*, *cuyos*, *cuyas*)
agrees in number and gender with the noun that follows
it and refers to people and things. *Cuyo* is never used as
an interrogative. *¿de quién...?* is used in its place. The
English equivalent of *cuyo* is *whose*.

Examples:

*París es una ciudad cuyos habitantes son muy
elegantes.*
Paris is a city whose residents are very elegant.

David es el dentista cuya madre es médica.
David is the student whose mother is a doctor.

Exercises: Translate the following sentences.

1. The young man with whom I was studying is
my cousin.

   _____

2. She wrote a letter to the man whom she met at
the beach.

   _____

3. Rosa is the student whose parents just got
divorced.

   _____

4. What he told me is not true.

   _____

5. The novelist who wrote *Maldito amor* is here.

   _____

6. The one who said that told the truth.

   _____

7. María spent a lot of money, which was not
necessary.

   _____

8. Susana is the one who called.

   _____

9. The young man who brought the records is a
lot of fun.

   _____

10. Do whatever you want.

   _____

13.4 Interrogative adjectives, pronouns, and adverbs

Interrogative adjectives modify a noun and ask a question. Interrogative pronouns ask about a person or thing
that has not been mentioned. Interrogative adverbs answer the questions *when*, *how*, *where*, and *why*.

13.4.1 Interrogative adjectives and pronouns

Interrogative adjectives and pronouns take an accent to
distinguish them from the same word when not used as
an interrogative. The interrogative adjectives are:

masculine		feminine		
singular	plural	singular	plural	
qué	qué	qué	qué	what, which
cuánto	cuántos	cuánta	cuántas	how much, how many
quién	quiénes	quién	quiénes	who
cuál	cuáles	cuál	cuáles	which

Examples:

¿Qué quieres?
What do you want?

¿Cuántas personas fueron a la conferencia?
How many people went to the conference?

Exercises: Translate into Spanish the interrogative adjectives and pronouns in parentheses.

1. ¿Sabes _____ asistieron a la reunión? (who)

2. Quiero saber _____ dijo Enrique. (what)

3. ¿_____ prefieres? ¿Los muebles antiguos o los nuevos? (Which)

4. ¿_____ años tiene la abuela de María Eugenia? (How many)

5. Desean enterarse de _____ pagó la cuenta. (who)

6. ¿_____ toallas compraste? (How many)

7. Dime _____ dinero te dio. (how much)

8. ¿_____ es tus hermano? (Which)

13.4.2 Uses of interrogative adjectives and pronouns

The interrogative adjectives and pronouns are used in the following manner:

a) *qué* may be used in front of nouns representing either persons or things. Its English equivalent is *what*. *Qué* is also used as an exclamation with the meaning of *what!*

Examples:

¿Qué persona no diría lo mismo?
What person wouldn't say the same?

¡Qué lujo!
What luxury!

b) *cuánto* means *how much* in the singular and *how many* in the plural. *Cuánto* may also be used as an exclamation and takes the form of *cuán* before adjectives and adverbs.

Examples:

¿Cuánto dinero ha traído?
How much money have you brought?

¡Cuánto habla!
He talks so much!

¡Cuán fácilmente escribe!
How easily she writes!

c) *quién* is used only as a pronoun and is restricted to *persons*.

Example:

¿Quién escribió?
Who wrote?

d) *cuál* is used with persons and things. *Cuál* takes the place of *qué* before the verb *to be*, except when a definition is required. *Cuál* implies an answer with numerous possibilities. It is always used before a phrase introduced by *de*.

Examples:

¿Cuál será la conclusión?
What will be the conclusion?

¿Qué es el amor?
What is (the meaning of) love?

¿Cuál de las dos quieres?
Which of the two do you want?

Exercises: Translate the following sentences.

1. How much he dances!

_____

2. What a report! It is excellent.

_____

3. What is fantasy?

_____

4. Who brought the compact disc?

_____

5. How easily he sings!

_____

6. Which of the European capitals do you prefer?

_____

13.4.3 Interrogative adverbs

Interrogative adverbs are similar to their adverbial form except for an accent on the syllable that has the spoken stress.

adverb of place	dónde*	where
adverb of time	cuándo	when
adverb of manner	cómo	how
adverb of cause	por qué	why

_____

*_a dónde_ asks about motion to a place, _de dónde_ asks about movement from a place, _en dónde_ asks about a stationary position, and _por dónde_ asks through where or how.

Examples:

¿Dónde está Margarita?
Where is Margarita?

¿A dónde vas?
Where are you going?

¿De dónde vienes?
Where are you coming from?

¿En dónde vives?
Where do you live?

¿Por dónde vas?
How are you going?

¿Cuándo vienes?
When are you coming?

¿Cómo estás?
How are you?

¿Por qué no fuiste?
Why didn't you go?

Exercises: Translate into Spanish the interrogative adverbs in parentheses.

1. ¿_____ vas a ir? (How)

2. ¿_____ no me llamaste anoche? (Why)

3. ¿_____ vienes? (From where)

4. ¿_____ lo hiciste? (How [manner])

5. Dime _____ él llegó. (when)

6. ¿_____ veranean tus padres? (Where)

7. ¿_____ fue Jorge? (Where)

8. ¿_____ lo supo? (How)

9. ¿_____ quieres ir? (When)

10. Explícale _____. (why)

✓ Check Yourself

13.1 (Possessive adjectives that precede nouns)

1. mis 2. Su 3. Tus 4. Nuestros 5. Vuestras 6. su 7. sus 8. mis 9. Su 10. Nuestras

13.1.1 (Possessive adjectives that follow nouns)

1. nuestra 2. mías 3. vuestros 4. suyo/de él 5. nuestros 6. suyo/de ella 7. vuestros 8. mío 9. nuestros 10. suyas/de ella

13.1.2 (Possessive pronouns)

1. los suyos 2. la mía 3. los míos 4. las tuyas 5. nuestros 6. la suya 7. las suyas 8. La nuestra 9. la suya 10. vuestros

13.2 (Demonstrative adjectives)

1. estos 2. Ese 3. Esas 4. Ese 5. Esta 6. esos 7. aquellos 8. este

13.2.1 (Demonstrative pronouns)

1. ésas 2. aquél 3. este 4. eso 5. aquélla 6. ésos

13.3.1 (Relative pronouns and their usages)

1. El joven con quien estudiaba es mi primo. 2. Ella le escribió una carta al hombre que conoció en la playa. 3. Rosa es la estudiante cuyos padres acaban de divorciarse. 4. Lo que me dijo no es verdad. 5. La novelista que escribió *Maldito amor* está aquí. 6. El que dijo eso, dijo la verdad. 7. María gastó mucho dinero, lo cual no era necesario. 8. Susana es la que llamó. 9. El joven que trajo los discos es muy divertido. 10. Haz/Haga lo que quieras/quiera.

13.4.1 (Interrogative adjectives and pronouns)

1. quiénes 2. qué 3. Cuáles 4. Cuántos 5. quién 6. Cuántas 7. cuánto 8. Cuál

13.4.2 (Uses of interrogative adjectives and pronouns)

1. ¡Cuánto baila! 2. ¡Qué informe! Es excelente. 3. ¿Qué es la fantasía? 4. ¿Quién trajo el disco compacto? 5. ¡Cuán fácilmente canta! 6. ¿Cuál de las capitales europeas prefieres?

13.4.3 (Interrogative adverbs)

1. Cómo 2. Por qué 3. De dónde 4. Cómo 5. cuándo 6. Dónde 7. A dónde 8. Cómo 9. Cuándo 10. por qué

Grade Yourself

Circle the numbers of the questions you missed, then fill in the total incorrect for each topic. If you answered more than three questions incorrectly, you need to focus on that topic. (If a topic has less than three questions and you had at least one wrong, we suggest you study that topic also. Read your textbook, a review book, or ask your teacher for help.)

Subject: Other Adjectives and Pronouns

Topic	Question Numbers	Number Incorrect
Possessive adjectives that precede nouns	**13.1:** 1, 2, 3, 4, 5, 6, 7, 8, 9, 10	
Possessive adjectives that follow nouns	**13.1.1:** 1, 2, 3, 4, 5, 6, 7, 8, 9, 10	
Possessive pronouns	**13.1.2:** 1, 2, 3, 4, 5, 6, 7, 8, 9, 10	
Demonstrative adjectives	**13.2:** 1, 2, 3, 4, 5, 6, 7, 8	
Demonstrative pronouns	**13.2.1:** 1, 2, 3, 4, 5, 6	
Relative pronouns and their usages	**13.3.1:** 1, 2, 3, 4, 5, 6, 7, 8, 9, 10	
Interrogative adjectives and pronouns	**13.4.1:** 1, 2, 3, 4, 5, 6, 7, 8	
Uses of interrogative adjectives and pronouns	**13.4.2:** 1, 2, 3, 4, 5, 6	
Interrogative adverbs	**13.4.3:** 1, 2, 3, 4, 5, 6, 7, 8, 9, 10	

Comparatives and Superlatives

Brief Yourself

Comparatives are used to compare adjectives, nouns, adverbs, and verbs and indicate an equal or unequal relationship between what is being compared. The superlative indicates the maximum or minimum degree of a particular quality. It is frequently used when comparing a person, place, or thing with a group. The group may be explicitly stated or simply implied.

Test Yourself

14.1 Comparisons of inequality

Spanish uses the following pattern to make comparisons of inequality with adjectives, nouns, and adverbs:

más/menos + adjective/noun/adverb + *que*

Examples:

Adjective: *María es más inteligente que Salvador.*
María is more intelligent than Salvador.

Noun: *Mi coche gasta menos gasolina que tu camioneta.*
My car uses less gas than your van.

Adverb: *Ella corre más rápidamente que su hermana.*
She runs faster than her sister.

Exercises: Write a logical comparison based on the information mentioned in each exercise using *más* and *menos que*.

1. Julián es muy alto. Erica es de estatura media.

   Julián _____.

2. Raúl siempre está solo. Josefina tiene muchos amigos.

   Raúl _____.

3. Teresa es muy religiosa. Juan nunca va a la iglesia.

   Teresa _____.

4. Carlos siempre está contando chistes cómicos. Rodolfo es serio.

   Carlos _____.

5. Alfredo es egoísta y sólo piensa en sí mismo. Laura es generosa y siempre ayuda a sus amigos.

   Alfredo _____.

6. Osvaldo es inteligente y siempre recibe buenas notas en sus clases. Héctor normalmente recibe malas notas.

   Osvaldo _____.

7. La señora Martínez es muy delgada. La señorita Pérez pesa demasiado para su estatura.

   La señora Martínez _____.

8. Andrés tiene tres hermanos. Su amiguito Miguel tiene dos.

   Miguel _____.

9. Javier nunca trabaja y es muy perezoso. Roberto trabaja todos los días.

   Javier_____.

10. Alejandro Plata tiene un millón de pesos. Olga Peseta sólo tiene treinta y nueve pesos.

    Olga _____.

11. La cumbia es muy difícil de bailar. El bolero más fácil de bailar.

    La cumbia _____ el bolero.

14.1.1 Comparisons of inequality with numerical expressions

The following pattern is used when quantity is mentioned.

más/menos + *de* + number

Examples:

Ayer leí más de tres artículos.
Yesterday I read more than three articles.

En menos de dos semanas, estaremos de vacaciones.
In less than two weeks, we will be on vacation.

Exercises: Complete the following sentences with the Spanish equivalent of the numerical expression in parentheses.

1. Fernando tiene _____ pesos. (less than twenty)

2. Rosario sacó _____ fotografías. (more than one hundred)

3. Antonio perdió _____ kilos. (more than ten)

4. No había _____ invitados. (more than five)

5. La biblioteca no te deja sacar _____ libros a la vez. (more than ten)

6. Pagamos_____ dólares de alquiler por el apartamento. (more than five hundred)

7. Hay_____millones de hispanos en EE.UU. (less than thirty)

8. El sueldo mínimo es_____dólares por hora. (less than five)

9. Trabajamos_____ horas por semana. (more than forty)

10. En América hay_____ países de habla española. (more than seventeen)

14.2 Comparisons of equality

Spanish uses comparisons of equality with nouns, verbs, and adjectives.

14.2.1 Comparisons of equality with nouns

To make comparisons of equality with nouns, use the following pattern:

tanto/a/os/as + noun + *como*

Note that *tanto*, *tanta*, *tantos*, and *tantas* agree in gender and number with the noun.

Examples:

Mi hermana tiene tantas faldas como yo.
My sister has as many skirts as I do.

Carmen cose tantos pantalones como Alberto.
Carmen sews as many pants as Alberto.

Exercises: Make comparisons of equality using the expressions *tanto*, *tanta*, *tantos*, and *tantas... como.*

1. Mario tiene ocho cuadros. Francisco tiene ocho cuadros también.

   Mario _____.

2. Susana trabaja ocho horas cada día. Diego trabaja ocho horas cada día.

   Susana _____.

3. Yo compro tres corbatas. Mi primo compra tres corbatas.

   Yo _____.

4. Durante el fin de semana vimos dos películas. Ustedes vieron dos películas también.

   Nosotros _____.

5. Dolores ganó 100.000 pesetas en la lotería. Germán ganó 100.000 pesetas en la lotería.

   Dolores _____.

6. Gabriel García Márquez recibió un premio Nóbel. Camilo José Cela también recibió un premio Nóbel.

   Gabriel García Márquez _____
   _____.

7. Alicia tiene dos amigas francesas. Amalia tiene dos amigas francesas.

   Alicia _____.

8. Pancho va a reparar cinco bicicletas. Orlando va a reparar cinco.

   Pancho _____.

9. En el restaurante Pollo Loco trabajan diez camareros. El café Colón tiene diez camareros.

   En el restaurante Pollo Loco _____
   _____.

10. Tomás bebe tres vasos de leche. Elena bebe tres vasos de leche.

    Tomás _____.

14.2.2 Comparisons of equality with verbs and adjectives

To make comparisons of equality with verbs, use the following pattern:

verb + *tanto como*

Examples:

Trabajo tanto como ella.
I work as much as she does.

Estudian tanto como nosotros.
They study as much as we do.

To make comparisons of equality with adjectives and adverbs, use the following pattern:

tan + adjective/adverb + *como*

Examples:

Él es tan hablador como mi amiga.
He is as talkative as my friend.

Conduzco tan rápidamente como tú.
I drive as rapidly as you do.

Exercises: Make logical comparisons of equality using either the expression *tanto como* or *tan...como.*

1. La señora García escribe dos cartas. El señor Ortíz escribe dos cartas.

   La señora García _____ el señor Ortíz.

2. Isabel maneja cuidadosamente. Rafael maneja con cuidado.

   Isabel _____ Rafael.

3. Los mariscos en Galicia son fantásticos. Los mariscos en Valencia son estupendos.

   Los mariscos en Galicia _____ los mariscos en Valencia.

4. Jorge chismea mucho con sus amigos. Anita también chismea con sus compañeras.

   Jorge_____ Anita.

5. Jesús es muy inteligente. Lourdes también es muy inteligente.

   Jesús _____ Lourdes.

6. La señorita Rodríguez plancha seis camisas. El señor López plancha seis camisas.

   La señorita Rodríguez _____ el señor López.

7. Juanito canta mal. Su hermano Rodolfo también canta mal.

   Juanito _____ Rodolfo.

8. Mi habitación está muy desorganizada. La habitación de mi compañera de apartamento también está muy desorganizada.

   Mi habitación _____ su habitación.

9. El Real Madrid ganó seis partidos de fútbol. El Deportivo de La Coruña ganó seis partidos.

   El Real Madrid _____ el Deportivo de La Coruña.

10. Los empleados están muy enojados. Su jefe también está muy enojado.

    Los empleados _____ su jefe.

Exercises: Make logical comparisons of equality or inequality for each situation.

11. Mario tiene seis libros. Pedro tiene seis libros.

    Mario _____ Pedro.

12. Eduardo corre cinco kilómetros cada día. Pepe corre siete kilómetros diarios.

    Eduardo _____ Pepe.

13. Isabel lee dos libros cada semana. Roberto lee dos libros por semana.

    Isabel _____ Roberto.

14. Augusto es muy popular. Emilio también conoce a mucha gente.

    Augusto _____ Emilio.

15. Modesto camina rápidamente. Miguel camina rápidamente.

    Modesto _____ Miguel.

16. Gabriela gana $30,000 al año. Jorge también gana $30,000.

    Gabriela _____ Jorge.

17. Marcos tiene dos pantalones negros. Yo tengo tres.

    Marcos _____ yo.

18. Luis es alto. Carlos también es alto.

    Luis _____ Carlos.

19. Nosotras trabajamos cinco días a la semana. Mis primos trabajan seis días cada semana.

    Nosotras _____ mis primos.

20. Escucho música todos los días. Ella también la escucha todos los días.

    Yo _____ ella.

14.2.3 Irregular comparatives

The adjectives *bueno*, *malo*, *viejo*, and *joven* have irregular forms in the comparative and superlative. Note that *más* and *menos* are not used with the following irregular forms:

bueno	mejor	better
viejo	mayor	older
malo	peor	worse
joven	menor	younger

Examples:

Ella prepara la paella mejor que su hermana.
She prepares paella better than her sister.

Mi padre es mayor que mi madre.
My father is older than my mother.

Exercises: Make the appropriate comparison using *mejor*, *peor*, *mayor*, or *menor*.

1. Miguel tiene treinta años. Manuel tiene veinte y dos años.

    Miguel _____ Manuel.

2. Los estudiantes en la escuela primaria tienen seis años. El profesor Ortíz tiene cuarenta y dos años.

    Los estudiantes _____ el profesor Ortíz.

3. Reynaldo es un buen jugador de baloncesto. José no es tan bueno.

    Reynaldo _____ José.

4. Mi coche no funciona bien. El coche de Ángel siempre funciona bien.

    Mi coche _____ el coche de Ángel.

5. Esta medicina cura más rápidamente que las otras.

    Esta medicina _____ las otras.

6. Pedro es un buen cantante. Juan no es tan bueno.

    Pedro _____ Juan.

14.3 Superlatives

The superlative indicates the highest degree of a particular quality.

14.3.1 Superlatives of adjectives

Superlatives of adjectives are frequently used when comparing persons, places, or things with a group that may be expressed explicitly or implied by the context. To form the superlative of an adjective, use the following pattern:

el/la/los/las + noun (optional) + *más* + adjective + *de* + group

Examples:

Mi hermana es la más rica de la familia.
My sister is the richest of the family.

Ellos son los más perezosos de toda la compañía.
They are the laziest of the whole company.

El Brasil es el país más grande de Sudamérica.
Brazil is the largest country in South America.

Exercises: Complete the following sentences, providing the Spanish equivalent for the words in parentheses.

1. La ciudad de México es _____ mundo. (the biggest)

2. Raúl es _____ atletas. (the strongest)

3. Esteban es _____ clase. (the most inquisitive)

4. Ana es _____ vendadoras. (the hardest working)

5. Esta silla es _____ todas. (the most comfortable)

6. Este examen fue _____ semestre. (the most difficult)

7. Aquella casa es _____ barrio. (the oldest)

8. Su novia es _____ chicas. (the prettiest)

9. Mi propuesta es _____ todas. (the most innovative)

10. Este ejercicio es _____ capítulo. (the easiest)

11. Octavio Paz es _____ poetas mexicanos contemporáneos. (the most famous)

14.3.2 Absolute superlative

The absolute superlative indicates the maximum degree of an adjective without any comparison to a group. Like all adjectives, the absolute superlative agrees in gender and number with the noun being modified. It is formed by adding the suffix *-ísimo, -ísima, -ísimos,* or *-ísimas* to the stem of an adjective. To form the stem for adjectives ending in a vowel, omit the final vowel and add the suffix.

adjective	stem	absolute superlative
guapo	guap-	guapísimo/a/os/as (extremely handsome)
inteligente	inteligent-	inteligentísimo/a/os/as (extremely smart)
bueno	buen-	buenísimo/a/os/as (extremely good)

Note that certain changes in spelling are necessary to maintain consistent pronunciation in the superlative form of the adjectives.

c	*qu*	
rico	riqu-	riquísimo /a/ os/ as
g	*gu*	
largo	largu-	larguísimo/a/os/as

Exercises: Complete the following sentences using the superlative form of the adjectives in parentheses.

1. Guillermo está _____ hoy. (contento)

2. La calle es _____. (estrecho)

3. Tengo un primo _____. (feo)

4. Las casas en este barrio son _____.
   (caro)

5. Mi tía es _____. (importante)

6. Los estudiantes siempre están
   _____. (cansados)

7. Mi abuelo tiene ciento dos años. Es
   _____. (viejo)

8. Los jugadores de baloncesto son _____.
   (alto)

9. Aquella actriz es _____. (famosa)

10. La comida está _____ hoy.
    (rico)

14.4 Indefinite and negative expressions

Indefinite expressions are used to refer to something or someone that is undetermined or unquantifiable. These expressions can be pronouns, adjectives, or adverbs.

a) indefinite expressions used as pronouns:

algo	something
alguien	someone
alguno/a/os/as	some
nada	nothing
nadie	no one
ninguno/a	none*

*Used in the singular and in the negative.

b) indefinite expressions used as adjectives:

algún/a/os/as	some
ningún, ninguna*	any

*Used in the singular and in the negative.

c) indefinite expressions used as adverbs:

siempre	always
alguna vez	ever, at some time
también	also
nunca, jamás	never
tampoco	neither

d) There are two ways to form negative sentences in Spanish. Keep in mind that *no* or a negative expression must always precede the verb.

no + verb + negative expression

Examples:

No encontré nada que me gustara.
I didn't find anything that I liked.

Nunca almuerzo antes de la una.
I never eat lunch before one o'clock.

Unlike in English, multiple negatives are used in Spanish.

Example:

Ella nunca habla mal de nadie.
She never speaks badly about anyone.

Nadie me dijo nada de ningún problema.
No one ever told me anything about any problem.

A personal *a* precedes *alguien* and *nadie* when they serve as direct objects.

Example:

Conozco a alguien que sabe tocar la gaita.
I know someone who knows how to play the bagpipe.

Exercises: Translate the following sentences using the appropriate indefinite and negative expressions.

1. No one is ever in the store after ten o'clock.

   _____

2. Gloria doesn't know him either.

   _____

3. There is no mail for anyone today.

   _____

4. Some of their ideas are interesting.

_____

5. Have you ever gone to Seville?

_____

Exercises: Answer the following questions negatively using negative expressions.

6. ¿Siempre desayunas a las siete?

_____

7. ¿Tienes algunas fotografías de tu viaje?

_____

8. ¿Ella tiene algo que decirle a alguien aquí?

_____

9. ¿Te gustaría probar algunas de las tapas?

_____

10. ¿Alguien les dijo algo a mis padres de lo que estamos haciendo?

_____

11. ¿Ellos van a pasar algunos días en Granada con algún amigo?

_____

12. ¿La empresa va a despedir a alguien?

_____

13. ¿Alguna vez has montado a caballo?

_____

14. ¿Ellos tienen que añadir algunas cifras más?

_____

15. ¿Hay alguien en casa?

_____

✓ Check Yourself

14.1 (Comparisons of inequality)

1. Julián es más alto que Erica. 2. Raúl tiene menos amigos que Josefina. 3. Teresa es más religiosa que Juan. 4. Carlos es más cómico que Rodolfo./Carlos es menos serio que Rodolfo. 5. Alfredo es más egoísta que Laura./Alfredo es menos generoso que Laura. 6. Osvaldo es más inteligente que Héctor. 7. La señora Martínez es más delgada que la señorita Pérez. 8. Miguel tiene menos hermanos que Andrés. 9. Javier es más perezoso que Roberto./Javier trabaja menos que Roberto. 10. Olga tiene menos pesos que Alejandro./Olga es menos rica/más pobre que Alejandro. 11. La cumbia es más difícil de bailar que el bolero.

14.1.1 (Comparisons of inequality with numerical expressions)

1. menos de veinte 2. más de cien 3. más de diez 4. más de cinco 5. más de diez 6. más de quinientos 7. menos de treinta 8. menos de cinco 9. más de cuarenta 10. más de diecisiete

14.2.1 (Comparisons of equality with nouns)

1. Mario tiene tantos cuadros como Francisco. 2. Susana trabaja tantas horas como Diego. 3. Yo compro tantas corbatas como mi primo. 4. Nosotros vimos tantas películas como ustedes. 5. Dolores ganó tanto dinero como Germán. 6. Gabriel García Márquez recibió tantos premios Nóbel como Camilo José Cela. 7. Alicia tiene tantas amigas francesas como Carmen. 8. Pancho va a reparar tantas bicicletas como Orlando. 9. En el restaurante Pollo Loco trabajan tantos camareros como en el café Colón. 10. Tomás bebe tantos vasos de leche como Elena.

14.2.2 (Comparisons of equality with verbs and adjectives)

1. escribe tanto como 2. maneja tan cuidadosamente como 3. son tan fantásticos como 4. chismea tanto como 5. es tan inteligente como 6. plancha tanto como 7. canta tan mal como 8. está tan desorganizada como 9. ganó tanto como 10. están tan enojados como 11. tiene tantos libros como 12. corre menos kilómetros que 13. lee tanto como/lee tantos libros como 14. es tan popular como/tiene tantos amigos como 15. camina tan rápidamente como 16. gana tanto como/gana tanto dinero como 17. tiene menos pantalones negros que 18. es tan alto como (mide tanto como) 19. trabajamos menos que/trabajamos menos horas que 20. escucho tanta música como

14.2.3 (Irregular comparatives)

1. es mayor que 2. son menores que 3. es mejor que 4. es peor que 5. es mejor que 6. es mejor cantante que

14.3.1 (Superlatives of adjectives)

1. la más grande del 2. el más fuerte de los 3. el más preguntón/curioso de la 4. la más trabajadora de las 5. la más cómoda de 6. el más difícil del 7. la más antigua del 8. la más guapa/hermosa/bonita de las 9. la más innovadora de 10. el más fácil del 11. el más famoso los

14.3.2 (Absolute superlative)

1. contentísimo 2. estrechísima 3. feísimo 4. carísimas 5. importantísima 6. cansadísimos 7. viejísimo 8. altísimos 9. famosísima 10. riquísima

14.4 (Indefinite and negative expressions)

1. Nunca hay nadie en la tienda después de las diez./No hay nadie nunca en la tienda después de las diez. 2. Gloria no lo conoce tampoco./Tampoco lo conoce Gloria. 3. No hay correo para nadie hoy. 4. Algunas de sus ideas son interesantes. 5. ¿Alguna vez has ido a Sevilla? 6. No, no desayuno nunca a las siete./No, nunca desayuno a las siete. 7. No, no tengo ninguna fotografía. 8. No, no tiene nada que decirle a nadie aquí. 9. No, no me gustaría probar ninguna tapa. 10. No, nadie les dijo nada a tus/sus padres de lo que estamos/están haciendo. 11. No, ellos no van a pasar ningún día en Granada con ningún amigo. 12. No, la empresa no va a despedir a nadie. 13. No, nunca he montado a caballo. 14. No, ellos no tienen que añadir ninguna cifra. 15. No, no hay nadie en casa./No, nadie está en casa.

Grade Yourself

Circle the numbers of the questions you missed, then fill in the total incorrect for each topic. If you answered more than three questions incorrectly, you need to focus on that topic. (If a topic has less than three questions and you had at least one wrong, we suggest you study that topic also. Read your textbook, a review book, or ask your teacher for help.)

Subject: Comparatives and Superlatives

Topic	Question Numbers	Number Incorrect
Comparisons of inequality	**14.1:** 1, 2, 3, 4, 5, 6, 7, 8, 9, 10, 11	
Comparisons of inequality with numerical expressions	**14.1.1:** 1, 2, 3, 4, 5, 6, 7, 8, 9, 10	
Comparisons of equality with nouns	**14.2.1:** 1, 2, 3, 4, 5, 6, 7, 8, 9, 10	
Comparisons of equality with verbs and adjectives	**14.2.2:** 1, 2, 3, 4, 5, 6, 7, 8, 9, 10, 11, 12, 13, 14, 15, 16, 17, 18, 19, 20	
Irregular comparatives	**14.2.3:** 1, 2, 3, 4, 5, 6	
Superlatives of adjectives	**14.3.1:** 1, 2, 3, 4, 5, 6, 7, 8, 9, 10, 11	
Absolute superlative	**14.3.2:** 1, 2, 3, 4, 5, 6, 7, 8, 9, 10	
Indefinite and negative expressions	**14.4:** 1, 2, 3, 4, 5, 6, 7, 8, 9, 10, 11, 12, 13, 14, 15	

Prepositions and Conjunctions

15

Brief Yourself

Prepositions are used to express the relationship that exists between things with respect to time and place. Conjunctions are words that function as connectors between words, phrases, clauses, or sentences.

Test Yourself

15.1 Prepositions

The most common prepositions in Spanish are:

a	to, at, in
ante	before, in the presence of
bajo	under, below
con	with
contra	against
de	of, from, by, about
delante	before
desde	from, since
durante	during
en	in, into, on, upon, at
entre	between, among
excepto	except
hacia	toward
hasta	as far as, to, up to, until
menos	except
para	for, to, in order to
por	for, by, to, through, on account of, per
salvo	except
según	according to
sin	without
sobre	on, upon, over, about
tras	after, behind, in pursuit of

Example:

La pareja caminó hacia el lago.
The couple walked toward the lake.

Exercises: Translate into Spanish the preposition in parentheses.

1. Carlos presentó el problema _____ gracia. (with)

2. Te quise conocer _____ que te vi. (since)

3. Hay que leer todos los documentos _____ éstos. (except)

4. _____ Josefina, la película era muy buena. (According to)

5. El hijo iba _____ el padre. (after, in pursuit of)

6. Vamos _____ el centro de la ciudad. (toward)

7. El presidente se presentó _____ los delegados. (before)

8. _____ el concierto, Luis se quedó dormido. (During)

9. El niño que está sentado _____ las dos señoras es mi vecino. (between)

10. Cristina puso el libro _____ la mesa. (on)

15.1.1 Special uses of some prepositions

The prepositions *a*, *de*, and *en* have several usages.

15.1.2 The preposition *a*

The preposition *a* is used in the following manner:

a) to indicate direction toward a point in space or a moment in time.

Example:

Voy a la iglesia.
I am going to church.

b) to indicate what took place at the end of a period of time.

Example:

A los dos meses de llegar aquí, conocí a Felipe.
Two months after I arrived, I met Felipe.

c) before an infinitive after verbs of motion.

Example:

Venimos a este club.
We come to this club.

d) *a* + *la* + feminine form of adjective and *a* + *lo* + masculine form of adjective indicate the manner in which something is done.

Examples:

Josefina cocina a la francesa.
Josefina cooks French style.

Se viste a lo japonés.
She dresses Japanese style.

e) *a* denotes manner or means by which something is done.

Example:

Lo hizo a regañadientes.
He did it reluctantly.

f) *a* expresses rate or price.

Example:

Lo vende a quince dólares el metro.
She sells it at fifteen dollars a meter.

g) *a* is used between two equal nouns.

Example:

paso a paso
step by step

h) *a* is used as *al* + infinitive to express simultaneous occurrences.

Example:

Vio a Pedro al llegar.
She saw Pedro on (upon) arriving.

i) *a* is used after the verbs *enseñar, aprender, comenzar, empezar,* and *llegar.* The infinitive follows *a.*

Example:

Mi padre me enseñó a nadar.
My father taught me to swim.

j) *a* is used before a direct object noun that refers to a specific person. It may also be used to personify an animal or a noun.

Examples:

Veo a mi amiga.
I see my friend.

Amo a mi país.
I love my country.

Exercises: Translate the following sentences into Spanish.

1. She wrote the documents one by one.

   _____

2. She likes to cook over a slow flame.

   _____

3. After being here two years, I obtained my degree.

   _____

4. She sells the oranges at 90¢ a dozen.

   _____

5. Juana cooks Cuban style.

   _____

6. I will see you at ten o'clock.

   _____

7. We are going to the party to have fun.

   _____

8. Upon hearing the news she became pale.

   _____

9. As soon as she arrived at her house she began to study.

   _____

10. They want to see María.

    _____

15.1.3 The preposition *de*

The preposition *de* is used in the following manner:

a) to indicate possession.

Example:

El libro es de Catalina.
The book belongs to Catalina.

b) to refer to the material of which something is made.

Example:

La casa es de madera.
The house is made out of wood.

c) to make reference to origin.

Example:

Los jóvenes son de Barcelona.
The young men are from Barcelona.

d) to indicate a specific time of the day.

Example:

Nos reuniremos a las ocho de la noche.
We will meet at eight o'clock P.M.

e) to describe personal characteristics.

Example:

El estudiante que conocí ayer es de ojos azules.
The student I met yesterday is blue-eyed.

f) after the superlative, and it has the English equivalent of *in*.

Example:

Pablo es el mejor de la familia.
Pablo is the best in the family.

g) as a synonym of *sobre* and *acerca*, and it has the *English equivalent about.*

Example:

Ustedes saben de todo.
You know (about) everything.

h) to mention the use for which a thing is intended.

Example:

Ésta es una máquina de escribir.
This is a typewriter.

i) to express cause.

Example:

Vino loco de alegría.
He came wild with joy.

j) to refer to manner of action or being.

Example:

Él sirvió de guía.
He served as a guide.

k) between the common noun and the proper names of countries, provinces, towns, islands, and geographical divisions.

Example:

el estrecho de Gibraltar
the strait of Gibraltar

Exercises: Translate the following sentences into Spanish.

1. She does not have a winter coat.

   _____

2. Ricardo is the worst athlete in his class.

   _____

3. The professor spoke about economics.

   _____

4. These horses belong to my family.

   _____

5. I forgot to bring the knitting needles.

   _____

6. He was filled with rage.

   _____

7. He visited the island of Cuba.

   _____

8. He worked as director of the company.

   _____

9. Camila is from Ecuador.

   _____

10. We go to the movies at three in the afternoon.

    _____

11. The black-haired woman is my aunt.

    _____

15.1.4 The preposition *en*

The preposition *en* is used in the following manner:

a) to refer to a definite place.

Example:

La vi en la playa.
I saw her at the beach.

b) as an equivalent of *on*.

Example:

Sofía estaba sentada en el sofá.
Sofía was seated on the sofa.

c) to indicate the means of transportation.

Example:

Me gusta viajar en tren.
I like to travel by train.

d) to refer to the way something is said.

Example:

Lo dijo en serio.
He said it seriously.

e) to indicate where an action is to take place.

Example:

La fiesta es en mi casa.
The party is at my house.

f) to refer to length of time.

Example:

Lo hizo en cinco horas.
He did it in five hours.

Exercises: Translate the following sentences into Spanish.

1. They are going by car to visit their relatives.

   _____

2. Alina finished the work in four minutes.

   _____

3. She said it jokingly.

   _____

4. I saw them at the lake.

   _____

5. Miguel had the ring on his finger.

   _____

6. The exhibit is at the Prado museum.

   _____

15.1.5 *Por* and *para*

The prepositions *por* and *para* sometimes have the English equivalent of *for*. Some usages of these prepositions are:

por is used in the following manner:

a) to indicate motion (through, along, by, via, around).

Examples:

Camino por el río.
I walk along the river.

Entró por la ventana.
He entered through the window.

Pasaré por tu casa a las cinco.
I'll come by your house at five o'clock.

b) to express agency, means, manner.

Example:

La llamaré por teléfono.
I will call her on the phone.

c) to indicate exchange.

Example:

Te doy $10.00 por el libro de historia.
I'll give you $10.00 for the history book.

d) in certain expressions. Some of these are *por ciento* and *por ahora.*

Example:

No puede ir por ahora.
He cannot go for now.

e) to indicate duration of time.

Example:

Estuvimos en la oficina del dentista por dos horas.
We were at the dentist's office for two hours.

f) to indicate approximate time in the future.

Example:

Los contratistas terminarán la construcción por enero.
The contractors will finish the construction around January.

g) to indicate *in search of* or *for*.

Example:

Vayan por el médico.
Go for the doctor.

h) with an infinitive to refer to an unfinished state.

Example:

Estoy por terminar la novela.
I am about to finish the novel.

i) with the passive voice to indicate the agent or cause.

Example:

Este libro fue escrito por la escritora mexicana Elena Garro.
This book was written by the the Mexican writer Elena Garro.

j) to express cause or motive of an action (because of, on account of, on behalf of).

Examples:

No fui a la fiesta por el trabajo que tenía que hacer.
I didn't go to the party because of the work that I had to do.

No llegamos a la boda a tiempo por la nieve.
We did not arrive at the wedding on time on account of the snow.

Margarita estaba enferma, yo trabajé por ella.
Margarita was sick; I worked in her place.

k) *por* + infinitive has the English equivalent of *for*, *because of*, and *for reason of*.

Example:

Perdimos la oportunidad de ir por llegar tarde.
We lost the opportunity to go because we arrived late.

para is used in the following manner:

a) to indicate destination in space.

Example:

Salimos para Madrid.
We are leaving for Madrid.

b) to refer to specific time in the future.

Example:

Ellos necesitan terminar la carta para las tres de la tarde.
They need to finish the letter by three in the afternoon.

c) to show direction toward a recipient.

Example:

Este regalo es para mi hermana Elena.
This gift is for my sister Elena.

d) with the infinitive to indicate *in order to*.

Example:

Vino para visitar a sus padres.
She came to visit her parents.

e) for comparisons. The English equivalents are *by the standard* and *considering*.

Example:

David es muy alto para su edad.
David is very tall for his age.

f) to indicate objective or goal.

Example:

Elisa e Isabel estudian para dentistas.
Elisa and Isabel are studying to become dentists.

g) to indicate a point of view.

Example:

Para mí, eso no es importante.
As for me, that is not important.

Exercises: Complete the following sentences with *por* or *para*.

1. Estuvimos en casa de Ofelia _____ cuatro horas.

2. El abuelo no se siente bien. Vayan _____ el médico.

3. Carolina le pidió el auto a su padre _____ ir al campo.

4. _____ no terminar a tiempo no pudimos ir.

5. Esto me lo dio Alicia _____ ti.

6. Salimos _____ Venezuela la semana que viene.

7. _____ mí, eso no es necesario.

8. Daniel y Micaela trabajan mucho _____ ahorrar dinero.

9. Este edificio fue diseñado _____ un arquitecto famoso.

10. La ciudad fue destruida _____ un terremoto.

11. La función del teatro empieza a las 7:00. Pasaré_____ ti a las 6:30.

12. El avión no pudo despegar _____ la tormenta.

13. El ministro está _____ entrar.

14. Hay que escribir el artículo _____ mañana.

15. Caminé _____ el parque anoche.

15.1.6 Compound prepositions

Compound prepositions are also known as prepositional phrases. Some common prepositional phrases are formed when:

a) an adjective is used adverbially and followed by *a*. For example:

concerniente	concerning
conforme a	according to
contrario a	contrary to
correspondiente a	corresponding to
frente a	opposite to

junto a	close to
respecto a	with respect to
tocante a	in/with regard to

b) simple adverbs are followed by *de*:

acerca de	about
además de	besides, in addition to
alrededor de	around
antes de	before (time, order)
cerca de	near, about
debajo de	under
delante de	before (place)
dentro de	within
después de	after
detrás de	behind, after (place)
encima de	over, on top of
fuera de	outside
lejos de	far from

c) prepositions precede adjectives used as adverbs and adverbs followed by *de*:

en cuanto a	as for
a causa de	on account of
a excepción de	with the exception of
a fuerza de	by dint of
a pesar de	in spite of, despite
a través de	across
con tal de	provided that
en frente de	in front of
en vez de	instead of
en virtud de	by virtue of
por causa de	by reason of

Exercises: Translate into Spanish the compound prepositions in parentheses.

1. Encontré el dinero _____ la cama. (under)

2. _____ al discurso, se ha logrado un tratado económico. (According to)

3. _____ lo que dice, él es un buen hombre. (In spite of)

4. El rector de la universidad llegará _____ la inauguración. (after)

5. _____ escribir una carta, llamó por teléfono. (Instead)

6. Le dieron una beca _____ su expediente académico. (in spite of)

7. Los parientes de Sofía viven _____ aquí. (far from)

8. Roberto dejó los guantes _____ la mesa. (on top of)

9. _____ la opinión pública, él fue un buen presidente. (Contrary to)

10. Margarita se sentó _____ su familia. (far from)

15.2   Conjunctions

A conjunction is a word that connects. The most common conjunctions are:

o (u before o or hom)	or
y (e before i or hi)*	and
pero, más, sino	but
ni	nor, neither
que	that
si	if, whether

_____
*y does not change before words beginning with *hie*, or with *y*.

Example:

Hablamos español e inglés.
We speak Spanish and English.

No quiero ni eso ni esto.
I want neither this nor that.

¿Vas con él o conmigo?
Are you going with him or with me?

Deseo seis u ocho manzanas.
I want six or eight apples.

Exercises: Translate the prepositions in parentheses.

1. ¿Qué desea? ¿Plata _____ oro? (or)

2. El mueble está hecho de madera _____ hierro. (and)

3. Es una asociación de padre _____ hijo. (and)

4. Necesitamos arroz _____ harina. (and)

5. Vienes ahora _____ te quedas aquí. (or)

15.2.1   Uses of *pero, sino, sino que*

The conjunctions *pero*, *sino*, and *sino que* have the English equivalent of *but*. These conjunctions are used in the following manner:

a) *pero* is used to join two independent clauses. If the first clause is affirmative, *pero* means *but*. If the first clause is negative, *pero* means *but* or *however*.

Examples:

Son buenos estudiantes, pero nunca estudian.
They are good students, but they never study.

No compré las entradas, pero podemos ir.
I didn't buy the tickets, but we can go.

b) *sino* means *but* when the first part of the sentence is negative and the second part contradicts the first. When a verb follows *sino*, the infinitive is used.

Examples:

No fuimos al cine, sino al concierto.
We didn't go to the movies, but to the concert.

No quiero estudiar, sino cantar.
I don't want to study, but (rather) sing.

c) *sino que* replaces *sino* when the clause that follows has a conjugated verb.

Example:

No la llevaron, sino que la trajeron.
They did not take it, but brought it.

Exercises: Complete the following sentences with *pero*, *sino*, or *sino que*.

1. Quiero regalarle uno de mis autos, _____ dice que no sabe conducir.

2. No le escribí una carta, _____ la llamé por teléfono.

3. No fueron a México, _____ al Canadá.

4. No he terminado mi trabajo, _____ puedo ayudarte.

5. Ella ya no es la quinta de su clase, _____ la primera.

6. No compró la casa, _____ la alquiló.

7. Llegué a tiempo, _____ ya se habían ido.

8. No la llevaron de compras, _____ la dejaron en casa.

9. No me lo vendió, _____ me lo regaló.

10. No quiere trabajar, _____ viajar.

✓ Check Yourself

15.1 **(Prepositions)**

1. con 2. desde 3. menos/salvo/excepto 4. Según 5. tras 6. hacia 7. ante 8. Durante 9. entre
10. en/sobre

15.1.2 **(The preposition *a*)**

1. Escribió los documentos uno a uno. 2. Le gusta cocinar a fuego lento. 3. A los dos años de estar aquí, obtuve mi título. 4. Ella vende las naranjas a 90¢ la docena. 5. Juana cocina a la cubana. 6. Te veré/veo a las diez. 7. Vamos a la fiesta a divertirnos. 8. Al escuchar la noticia palideció. 9. Tan pronto llegó a su casa empezó a estudiar. 10. Quieren ver a María.

15.1.3 **(The preposition *de*)**

1. Ella no tiene un abrigo de invierno. 2. Ricardo es el peor atleta de su clase. 3. El profesor habló de economía. 4. Estos caballos son de mi familia. 5. Se me olvidó traer las agujas de tejer. 6. Estaba lleno de ira. 7. Visitó la isla de Cuba. 8. Trabajó de director de la compañía. 9. Camila es de Ecuador.
10. Vamos al cine a las tres de la tarde. 11. La mujer de pelo negro es mi tía.

15.1.4 **(The preposition *en*)**

1. Van en coche a visitar a sus parientes. 2. Alina terminó el trabajo en cuatro minutos. 3. Lo dijo en broma. 4. Los vi en el lago. 5. Miguel tenía el anillo en el dedo. 6. La exposición es en el Museo del Prado.

15.1.5 **(*Por* and *para*)**

1. por 2. por 3. para 4. Por 5. para 6. para 7. Para 8. para 9. por 10. por 11. por 12. por 13. por
14. para 15. por

15.1.6 **(Compound prepositions)**

1. debajo de 2. Conforme 3. A pesar de 4. después de 5. En vez de 6. a pesar de 7. lejos de
8. encima de 9. Contrario a 10. lejos de

15.2 **(Conjunctions)**

1. u 2. y 3. e 4. y 5. o

15.2.1 **(Uses of *pero, sino, sino que*)**

1. pero 2. sino que 3. sino 4. pero 5. sino 6. sino que 7. pero 8. sino que 9. sino que 10. sino

Grade Yourself

Circle the numbers of the questions you missed, then fill in the total incorrect for each topic. If you answered more than three questions incorrectly, you need to focus on that topic. (If a topic has less than three questions and you had at least one wrong, we suggest you study that topic also. Read your textbook, a review book, or ask your teacher for help.)

Subject: Prepositions and Conjunctions

Topic	Question Numbers	Number Incorrect
Prepositions	**15.1:** 1, 2, 3, 4, 5, 6, 7, 8, 9, 10	
The preposition *a*	**15.1.2:** 1, 2, 3, 4, 5, 6, 7, 8, 9, 10	
The preposition *de*	**15.1.3:** 1, 2, 3, 4, 5, 6, 7, 8, 9, 10, 11	
The preposition *en*	**15.1.4:** 1, 2, 3, 4, 5, 6	
Por and *para*	**15.1.5:** 1, 2, 3, 4, 5, 6, 7, 8, 9, 10, 11, 12, 13, 14, 15	
Compound prepositions	**15.1.6:** 1, 2, 3, 4, 5, 6, 7, 8, 9, 10	
Conjunctions	**15.2:** 1, 2, 3, 4, 5	
Uses of *pero, sino, sino que*	**15.2.1:** 1, 2, 3, 4, 5, 6, 7, 8, 9, 10	

The Passive Voice

16

Brief Yourself

A sentence is in the *active voice* if the subject acts upon an object and is in the *passive voice* when a thing or a person is acted upon by an agent.

Test Yourself

16.1   The passive voice with an agent

The passive voice with an agent is formed with the auxiliary verb *ser* plus a past participle. The subject in the active sentence becomes the agent in the passive sentence. The direct object of the active sentence becomes the subject in the passive sentence. The verb in the active sentence takes a compound form formed by *ser* (in the same mood and tense of the verb in the active sentence), and a past participle that agrees with the new subject in gender and number.

Example:

Active voice:

Cervantes escribió la primera novela moderna.
Cervantes wrote the first modern novel.

In this sentence the subject *Cervantes* performs the action of the verb *escribió*. Both the verb and the sentence are in the active voice.

Passive voice:

*La primera novela moderna fue escrita por
   Cervantes.*
The first modern novel was written by Cervantes.

The above verb *fue escrita* and the sentence are in the passive voice. The passive subject *la primera novela moderna* receives the action of the passive verb *fue escrita*. The action is performed by the agent *Cervantes*.

Passive sentences with an agent are not very common in spoken Spanish.

Exercises: Fill in the blanks with the translation of the verbs in parentheses.

1. Los exámenes _____
    por el asistente del profesor. (will be corrected)

2. Los manifestantes ya _____ por
    la policía. (had been arrested)

3. Esta carta _____ por el
    nuevo jefe. (has been written)

4. El acuerdo diplomático _____
    por ambas embajadoras. (will be signed)

5. Las notificaciones de despido
    _____ anónimamente entre
    los empleados. (have been distributed)

6. Esa película también _____
    por Colomo. (was directed)

7. La casa _____ directamente
    por sus dueños. (was sold)

8. Las decisiones _____
   por expertos. (were made)

9. Las primeras ciudades de EE.UU.
   _____ por los españoles.
   (were founded)

10. Para mañana los problemas ya
    _____. (will have
    been solved)

11. El nuevo empleado _____
    constantemente por el supervisor. (was
    watched)

12. El extranjero _____
    injustamente. (was criticized)

13. La nueva ley de inmigración
    _____ por el congreso.
    (was approved)

14. Este libro _____ por dos
    profesores. (was written)

16.1.1 The passive voice without an agent

A sentence in the passive voice without an agent becomes impersonal and the action is generalized instead of being limited by a particular agent. Passive sentences without an agent are more common in Spanish than those with an agent. They are not as frequently used as in English.

Example:

San Agustín, la primera ciudad de EE.UU., fue fundada en 1565.
Saint Agustine, the first city in the U.S., was founded in 1565.

Exercises: Fill in the blanks with the Spanish translation of the verbs in parentheses.

1. Los cheques _____ ayer.
   (were sent)

2. El automóvil ya _____
   cuando llegamos. (had been repaired)

3. La mudanza de apartamento _____
   la semana pasada. (was made)

4. La fiesta _____ el sábado
   pasado. (was announced)

5. El presupuesto _____ sin
   ninguna notificación. (was cut)

6. Todos los documentos _____
   en el incendio. (were destroyed)

7. La autopista _____ en
   menos de un año. (was built)

8. Sin diálogo los problemas nunca
   _____. (will never be resolved)

9. Los regalos _____ gratuitamente
   a todos los estudiantes. (will be distributed)

10. Los trabajadores que protestaron
    _____. (were fired)

16.1.2 *Estar* used with the past participle

Estar is used with a past participle that serves as an adjective to focus upon the result of an action or a condition of the subject.

Examples:

Las tiendas están cerradas de dos a cuatro.
The stores are closed from two to four.

El museo está cerrado por remodelaciones.
The museum is closed for remodeling.

Exercises: Fill in the blanks with the translation of the verbs in parentheses.

1. El libro _____ en
   portugués. (is written)

2. Las tiendas _____ desde la
   mañana temprano. (are open)

3. La mesa _____ de madera. (is made)

4. Los exámenes _____ desde ayer. (are corrected)

5. Todos los problemas ya _____. (are solved)

6. Los ejercicios ya _____. (are done)

7. Los carros_____ en la calle. (are parked)

8. Todos los cuadros ya _____ de antemano. (are sold)

9. El automóvil ya _____. (is fixed)

10. Estos artículos _____ del portugués. (are translated)

11. Todos _____ con la variedad de comidas. (were satisfied)

12. El puesto ya _____. (is occupied)

16.1.3 The impersonal passive with *se*

The impersonal passive with *se* is the most common way of expressing the passive in Spanish. It is formed with *se* + the third person of the verb in any tense. The third person singular or plural is used, depending on the subject that follows the verb. The agent is not mentioned.

Examples:

En Miami se habla español por todas partes.
In Miami Spanish is spoken everywhere.

Últimamente se venden muchos discos compactos.
Lately many compact discs are sold.

Exercises: Fill in the blanks with the the translation of the expression in parentheses.

1. _____ bien en España. (One lives)

2. La cena _____ muy tarde en Bolivia. (is served)

3. En los Estados Unidos_____ comúnmente que América es un país. (people think)

4. En las fiestas latinas _____, _____ y _____. (people dance, talk, and drink)

5. Las casas _____ muy baratas este año. (are being sold)

6. Cada vez _____ más español en Norteamérica. (people speak)

7. Últimamente_____ fumar en los locales públicos. (is prohibited)

8. Más edificios _____ si _____. (will be built, they are are needed)

9. _____diferentemente de como _____. (One talks, one writes)

10. La ceremonia _____ a medianoche. (was closed)

11. _____ y _____ que los políticos son corruptos. (It is said, it is known)

12. _____ aumentar la matrícula. (It has been decided)

13. _____ mucho y _____ poco. (People talk, do)

14. Este libro _____ hace pocos años. (was published)

✓ Check Yourself

16.1 (The passive voice with an agent)

1. serán corregidos 2. habían sido arrestados 3. ha sido escrita 4. será firmado 5. han sido distribuidas 6. fue dirigida 7. fue vendida 8. fueron hechas 9. fueron fundadas 10. habrán sido resueltos 11. era vigilado 12. fue criticado 13. fue aprobada 14. fue escrito

16.1.1 (The passive voice without an agent)

1. fueron enviados 2. había sido reparado 3. fue hecha 4. fue anunciada 5. fue disminuido 6. fueron destruidos 7. fue construida 8. serán resueltos 9. serán distribuidos 10. fueron despedidos

16.1.2 (*Estar* used with the past participle)

1. está escrito 2. están abiertas 3. está hecha 4. están corregidos 5. están resueltos 6. están hechos 7. están estacionados 8. están vendidos 9. está reparado 10. están traducidos 11. estaban satisfechos 12. está ocupado

16.1.3 (The impersonal passive with *se*)

1. Se vive 2. se sirve 3. se piensa 4. se baila, se habla, se bebe 5. se venden 6. se habla 7. se prohíbe 8. se construirán, se necesitan 9. Se habla, se escribe 10. se clausuró 11. Se dice, se sabe 12. Se ha decidido 13. Se habla, se hace 14. se publicó

Grade Yourself

Circle the numbers of the questions you missed, then fill in the total incorrect for each topic. If you answered more than three questions incorrectly, you need to focus on that topic. (If a topic has less than three questions and you had at least one wrong, we suggest you study that topic also. Read your textbook, a review book, or ask your teacher for help.)

Subject: *The Passive Voice*

Topic	Question Numbers	Number Incorrect
The passive voice with an agent	**16.1:** 1, 2, 3, 4, 5, 6, 7, 8, 9, 10, 11, 12, 13, 14	
The passive voice without an agent	**16.1.1:** 1, 2, 3, 4, 5, 6, 7, 8, 9, 10	
Estar used with the past participle	**16.1.2:** 1, 2, 3, 4, 5, 6, 7, 8, 9, 10, 11, 12	
The impersonal passive with *se*	**16.1.3:** 1, 2, 3, 4, 5, 6, 7, 8, 9, 10, 11, 12, 13, 14